Nove

To Munk Steini

In appreciation for all your
caring help and for being a
Real mensch. Gratefully and
Cordially

Sare b. Dash

THE INTRUDERS

THE INTRUDERS

Unreasonable

Searches and

Seizures from

King John to

John Ashcroft

Samuel Dash

Rutgers University Press
New Brunswick, New Jersey, and London

Library of Congress Cataloging-in-Publication Data

Dash, Samuel.
The intruders : unreasonable searches and seizures from King John to
John Ashcroft / Samuel Dash.
p. cm.
Includes bibliographical references and index.
ISBN 0–8135–3409–7 (hardcover : alk. paper)
1. Searches and seizures—United States.—History. 2. Searches and seizures—England—History. I. Title.
KF9630 . D37 2004
345 . 73′0522—dc22
CIP

2003018835

British Cataloging-in-Publication information for this book is available from the British Library.

Manufactured in the United States of America

If a man makes a breach into a house, one shall kill him in front of the breach, and bury him in it.

Article 21, Code of Hammurabi, king of Babylonia, eighteenth century B.C.E.

A man's home is his castle.

Justinian, emperor of Rome, sixth century C.E.

CONTENTS

ACKNOWLEDGMENTS

I am greatly indebted to my colleagues at Georgetown University Law Center—Professors Daniel R. Ernst, James C. Oldham, and Louis Michael Seidman—for reading and editing my manuscript within the areas of their expertise and giving me valuable recommendations for correction and improvement. The historical and legal materials have benefited much from their help. They are not responsible, however, for the positions I take on these matters in this book. In addition, I am thankful to Justice Randy Holland of the Delaware Supreme Court for his many helpful suggestions.

The research for this book took several years and could not have been accomplished without the skillful and committed help of my law student research assistants during this period. I owe special thanks to these gifted former students: Max Bolstad, Stephen Campbell, Pat Casey, Audrey L. Harris, Ann Hart, K. Kathleen Kern, Christopher P. Reid, Manuel S. Varela, and Stacey L. Wruble.

In addition, this was a family project. As always, my wife, Sara, encouraged and inspired me to complete the book, although the work separated us too often. Also she read all the drafts of my manuscript and questioned and aided me constantly on style and structure. Through her guidance, I hope I have been able to translate legal concepts more clearly for the understanding of nonlawyers. My daughter Judi Ellen and her husband, David Molineaux, gifted writers in their own right, provided helpful suggestions for improvement of the writing. Finally, my daughter Rachel, a professor of family therapy and passionate believer in equal justice, added her talents to make the book more readable.

I am grateful to my secretarial assistant, Édeanna Johnson, who edited and put the book together for me in the proper style for publication. Lastly, I thank Marlie Wasserman, director of Rutgers University Press, for believing in me and my book and paving the way for its publication, as well as the staff members of the Press for all their help.

THE INTRUDERS

PROLOGUE

The poorest man may, in his cottage, bid defiance to all the forces of the
Crown. It may be frail; its roof may shake; the wind may blow through it; the storm may
enter; the rain may enter; but the King of England may not enter; all his force dare not
cross the threshold of the ruined tenement.

William Pitt, in the House of Commons, 1766

A little more than two hundred years after Pitt made this remarkable
declaration in Parliament, the force of a U.S. president unlawfully
broke into the homes and offices of private citizens, searched for and
seized their private papers, and wiretapped and bugged their private conversations. By then, the country was approaching the two hundredth
anniversary of the Fourth Amendment to the United States
Constitution, which proclaims, "The right of the people to be secure in
their persons, houses, papers, and effects against unreasonable searches
and seizures shall not be violated."

Richard Nixon's violations of the Fourth Amendment and his
betrayal of public trust in his obstructions of justice to cover up his crimes
are branded for all times under the label of "Watergate." They so shocked
the people of the United States that millions of them responded in written protests of outrage to the White House and to Congress. That protest
and the articles of impeachment approved by the House Judiciary
Committee led to the unprecedented resignation of the president.

When the Senate Watergate Committee held televised public hearings
on the Watergate scandal in the summer of 1973, John Ehrlichman, second

in command in the White House staff, was called as a witness before the Committee. He adamantly argued that the president of the United States had the power and authority to order burglaries and unwarranted searches of private homes and business offices. He testified, for example, that the break-in of the Los Angeles office of the psychiatrist of Daniel Ellsberg, who had leaked the Pentagon Papers, by G. Gordon Liddy and his burglary team was within the lawful power of the president.

Senator Herman Talmadge of Georgia took his turn at questioning Ehrlichman. He challenged Ehrlichman's assertion that the president can authorize burglaries and searches of houses without warrants and asked, "Do you remember when we were in law school, we studied a famous principle of law that came from England and also is well known in this country, that no matter how humble a man's cottage is, that even the King of England cannot enter without his consent?" With a snide smile, Ehrlichman replied, "I am afraid that has been considerably eroded over the years, has it not?" Talmadge shot back, "Down in my country we still think it is a pretty legitimate principle of law." The Senate Caucus Room exploded in applause.[1]

Ehrlichman was correct, in fact. The right of the people to be secure in their persons and homes against unreasonable searches and seizures, embodied in the Fourth Amendment, had been considerably eroded. At the time when Nixon was asserting presidential prerogative to defy constitutional protections of the people against unlawful searches and seizures, the Supreme Court's new majority, led by Warren Burger, whom Nixon had recently appointed as chief justice, was dismantling the body of law the Court had developed over the preceding twenty years to enforce Fourth Amendment protections.

The Court's narrowing of Fourth Amendment protections contradicted fundamental American principles of liberty and privacy. Indeed, it ignored one of the principal causes for the American colonies' revolt against England—the colonists' hatred of the unreasonable searches of their homes and shops ordered by King George III and executed by his colonial governors and judges. The Americans believed with a passion that they were being denied the rights of Englishmen under the Magna Carta, and they chose independence to secure these rights for themselves rather than submit to the tyranny of George III.

They were wrong in their belief that their fellow Englishmen at home enjoyed greater rights of privacy. Even when Pitt spoke in 1766, he was asserting a myth. The king of England and all his force could and did enter the homes and shops of his subjects, and arguably, unlike Nixon, he did so lawfully. The principle of security and privacy enshrined in Pitt's words and in the maxim "every man's home is his castle" was no more than an aspiration in eighteenth-century England. For Americans, it took the courage to fight a dangerous revolution against England and the insistence on a Bill of Rights to transform the aspiration for freedom from arbitrary government intrusion into the guarantee of fundamental law.

Watergate proved how fragile was this fundamental law. Under the slogan of patriotism and the protection of American freedom from subversives, President Nixon and his aides ran roughshod over that freedom and trampled on the right of the people to be secure in their homes and private conversations. Only the constitutional separation of powers doctrine, as implemented through congressional investigation, stopped Nixon in his tracks. The exposure by the Senate of what their government had done to their freedom protections outraged the American people, and the unprecedented response from Americans led to the resignation of the president. It was a scary time in the United States, and there was a collective sigh of relief from every part of the country when this effort to destroy our constitutional freedom failed.

Now, thirty years after Watergate, a very real threat to American freedom—international terrorism—has once again tested the durability of our constitutional liberty and free society. On September 11, 2001, when fanatic al Qaeda terrorists hijacked U.S. commercial airliners and crashed them into both towers of the World Trade Center in New York, into the Pentagon in Virginia, and into the ground in Pennsylvania after a passenger rebellion prevented an attack on the Capitol or the White House, we in this country felt complete vulnerability to surprise destruction any time and anywhere.

Over three thousand human beings were slaughtered in these attacks. President George W. Bush expressed the thoughts of most Americans when he announced a war against terrorism and an armed retaliation against Osama Bin Laden, his al Qaeda forces, and his Taliban supporters. That war in Afghanistan, supported by the United Nations, destroyed the Taliban government, killed many of the al Qaeda terrorists, and sent Osama Bin Laden and the rest of his followers into hiding. Two years later, without United Nations approval, President Bush ordered a preemptive war against the Saddam Hussein regime in Iraq, claiming it had ties with the al Qaeda terrorists and had weapons of mass destruction ready to use against the United States. Although an overwhelming American military force destroyed that regime, the president announced that the war on terrorism was not over.

War, yes, but at what price to constitutional liberties? War necessarily puts strain on individual rights, and the people accept this as a reasonable limitation on constitutional liberty. But how much liberty should the people surrender? We are dependent on the good judgment of our government, but as the lesson of history has shown, we cannot abdicate this crucial question to the government alone. It is imperative that we hold government accountable to maintain basic U.S. liberties. For what does America win if, in the fight against terrorism to preserve American freedom, the government deems it necessary to destroy that freedom?

This is not an academic or hypothetical question. The attorney general has already begun to dismantle some of the basic ingredients of our Bill of Rights protections. Frustrated by the difficult problems of detecting and preventing terrorist attacks on this country, he has been impatient over the restraints of the Fourth Amendment protections against unreasonable searches and seizures. He has recommended and obtained from Congress some frightening expansions of federal law enforcement's power to search, intrude on privacy, and conduct electronic surveillance. Disturbingly, like President Nixon, he has used the slogans of patriotism and protection of American freedoms to support his efforts to erode these freedoms. Worse yet, the government does not even need these expanded powers. As we shall see in later chapters, Congress and the Supreme Court have already, prior to 9/11, given the government all the authority and power it needs to fight terrorism.

In the spirit of cooperation to aid the war effort, most Americans have hesitated to question or protest against these limitations on individual rights. As shown during the period leading up to Nixon's abuse of power, the danger of passive acceptance is the loss of constitutional liberty by default. There is also the danger of the people taking the wonders of our constitutional free society too much for granted. We attained our freedom at a remarkable time in history through the vision of extraordinary leaders who invented a unique form of democratic government based on the sovereignty of the people, unequaled at any other time in world history.

An essential pillar of this free society is the constitutional protection against unreasonable searches and seizures. The ancient and sacred right of personal privacy was thought by the leaders of the American Revolution to have been recognized in the Magna Carta. To them, it was embedded in those certain inalienable rights of the people, endowed by their creator, to life, liberty, and the pursuit of happiness proclaimed in the Declaration of Independence. They demonstrated this belief by recognizing a preexisting right in the Fourth Amendment, not one created by the Constitution itself. The Fourth Amendment in the Bill of Rights begins with the words "The right of the people."

The Fourth Amendment is still vitally important to Americans today, though we live in a democracy and are not threatened by the tyranny of kings or dictators. One reason is that this protection of the privacy of our persons, homes, and offices from arbitrary government intrusion is part of our heritage from the Revolutionary War and the creation of our free nation. The Fourth Amendment has molded the character of the American people and the quality of our democratic government. It has symbolized the uniqueness of American freedom and the centrality of the concept of the rule of law and the sovereignty of the people.

Although the protections of the Fourth Amendment are no less sacred and necessary to our free society today than they were at the time Americans fought and died for them in the Revolutionary War, our passion for them seems to have cooled in modern America. So much so that many state and federal law enforcement officers today throughout the country feel free to ignore the constitutional limitations on their arrest and search powers. Frequently these officers are supported in these violations by fearful citizens, government leaders, judges, and legislators, who encourage law enforcement officers to fight an aggressive "war on crime." These groups have seemingly been unaware of how unsuccessful the crime warriors have been for reasons other than individual rights and how much they have sacrificed our freedom rights on a wasteful and unsupported strategy.

Many Americans today are subjected to illegal arrests and illegal searches in the name of effective crime fighting. Most victims are poor and minority members of American society. A big-city police chief once brazenly stated he would continue to order his officers to make unlawful street searches in poor neighborhoods where the residents were mostly African Americans. He boasted that random stops and searches of individuals and cars may be illegal, but they were popular, and his officers had confiscated large quantities of guns and knives by such unlawful procedures.[2]

A U.S. attorney general once wrote to a federal judge who had complained to him about discriminatory searches of black Americans that it was probably true that police stopped and searched more black people than white people. He justified this practice by claiming that it was also true that most street crimes were committed by black people, and their arrests served the "useful purpose of exposing them to the rehabilitative opportunities in the nation's prisons."[3]

More than two hundred years after ringing the Liberty Bell in celebration of American independence, it seems that our passion for liberty has indeed cooled. We still claim that we cherish our privacy in our homes, papers, and persons. However, we also have taken this right of privacy for granted because most of us have not had reason personally to fear unreasonable government intrusion. For the most part, we have not been concerned over the many illegal government searches and seizures committed frequently all around us. We have accepted, apparently, law enforcement officials' rationalization that, on balance, fighting crime, and now terror, should be considered by the people to have a greater priority than some "technicalities" in the Bill of Rights.

In recent times, the majority of the U.S. Supreme Court justices have accepted this law enforcement position. Their opinions have continuously reduced the protections of the Fourth Amendment to the extent that in most cases today, evidence seized in violation of that amendment is welcomed in evidence by courts. At the same time, the officers who acted unlawfully are rewarded and promoted for their crime-busting achievements. Such indifference to Fourth Amendment protections demonstrates how far we have drifted from Patrick Henry's cry, "Give me liberty or give me death." Alarmingly, it reveals popular complacence to constitutional abuses in the name of public safety.

Yet, how dangerous and foolish this trend is! The Founding Fathers warned against such complacency. By their example, they proved for all time that the liberty rights crucial to a free society and guaranteed in the Fourth Amendment have to be fought for against a powerful government. These rights were won for all Americans with great difficulty.

Once won, however, the founders knew that these human rights would remain constantly threatened, even in a democracy, by government intolerance or impatience. They trusted the people to be always vigilant to detect government encroachment on their liberty rights and to be ready to fight for them. They also knew that if these rights are lost, the lesson of history teaches that it is extremely difficult, if even possible, to obtain them again.

The human yearning for privacy is very ancient, and history reflects the bitterness of those millions in past times who lost personal privacy through government abuse. The desire for protection of private enjoyment of home and thought from arbitrary intrusion can be faintly sensed in the books of Genesis and Joshua in the Old Testament. The drunken and unruly crowd in Sodom that sought to seize the angels who were visiting Lot in search of ten honest men just before the city was destroyed did not break into Lot's house to get at the strangers, but first demanded that Lot bring them out of the house.[4]

When Jacob fled with his wives and his cattle from his father-in-law Laban's house, his wife Rachel stole her father's idols without Jacob's knowledge. Laban gave chase and caught up with Jacob, accusing him of the theft. Jacob consented to Laban's search of his tents. Rachel had hidden the idols under her camel saddle in her tent and sat on it when her father came to her tent to search. "Forgive me for not rising, my lord," she said, "but the woman's custom is on me." Laban refrained from disturbing her and, of course, searched her tent in vain.[5]

When the king of Jericho learned that Joshua's spies were being sheltered by Rachab the harlot, he did not dispatch a search party to enter Rachab's house to seize the spies. Instead, he sent a message to Rachab to produce them, giving Rachab the opportunity to conceal the spies and throw their pursuers off the track.[6]

When God complained to Joshua that Acham, one of his soldiers, had stolen part of the spoils of Jericho that had been consecrated to the

treasury of the House of the Lord, Joshua showed remarkable restraint.
He did not order a search of Acham's tent until after Acham had been
summoned from his tent to appear before Joshua and had confessed to
the stealing of the treasure and burying it under the floor of his tent.[7]
These biblical accounts have been interpreted as evidencing, even
at that ancient time, a respect by people—including rulers—for the sanctity of the home.[8] At the most, however, they represent only acts of discretion, not a recognition of an individual right. There is nothing in
ancient law that would have prohibited the king of Jericho from sending
his soldiers into Rachab's house to seize the spies or Joshua from immediately commanding a search of Acham's tent.

While ancient law did not limit a king's power to invade private
homes, it did make the home sacred against intrusion by ordinary individuals. Article 21 of the Code of Hammurabi, a contemporary of the
patriarchs of the Bible, declared: "If a man makes a breach into a house,
one shall kill him in front of the breach, and bury him in it."[9] This special protection of the home from private intrusion had strong religious
support. From earliest times homes were believed to be protected by
household gods, and unauthorized entries constituted acts of sacrilege
against those gods.

This belief that the home was holy was strong in ancient Greece
and, later, Rome. It led to the home being considered under certain circumstances to be a sanctuary like the temple. Cicero emphasized the
sacredness of the home when he declared, "What is more inviolate, what
better defended by religion than the house of a citizen. . . . This place of
refuge is so sacred to all men, that to be dragged from thence is unlawful." Indeed, it was Roman law, not English law, that first proclaimed the
protection of the home in the maxim "Every man's home is his castle."[10]

Even so, the Roman home was not free from search and seizure.
The Roman emperor could, at will, order searches of the homes of any
Roman citizen. Private persons also could obtain permission to search

another's home under appropriate procedures provided by Roman law. Interestingly, those procedures, particularly in criminal cases, anticipated some of the protective restrictions required by the U.S. Constitution today.[11]

This history should resonate in the hearts of all Americans. It should result in a sense of outrage over what Supreme Court Justice Louis D. Brandeis called "government law breaking," the same kind of outrage that led millions of Americans watching the Senate Watergate hearings in 1973 to write to and call the White House and Congress, protesting the illegal wiretapping, burglaries, and obstructions of justice authorized and participated in by Nixon.

We cannot fully appreciate the importance of the Fourth Amendment to free Americans without looking back on the saga of the struggle of all people throughout history to be free from arbitrary government intrusion. As we have seen, the story is very old and has its roots in biblical, Greek, and Roman times. Indeed, the English tradition of privacy in the home may have come from the Roman law brought by the Roman legions when they invaded and governed Britain. However, we begin our story in the thirteenth century, the time to which English legend traces the principle that every man's home is a castle that even the king may not enter. The date is June 15, 1215. The place, Runnymede, a green meadow south of London along the Thames between Windsor Castle and the town of Staines. It was there that the rebellious barons of the realm forced a submissive King John to accept the Magna Carta.

CHAPTER 1

The Legend of the Magna Carta

No free man shall be taken, imprisoned, disseised, outlawed, banished,
or in any way destroyed, nor will we proceed or prosecute against him except by the
lawful judgment of his peers and by the law of the land.

King John's promise to the barons at Runnymede in Magna Carta,
Chapter 39, June 15, 1215

Baron Robert Fitz-Walter, Lord of Dunmow and standard-bearer of the city of London, buried the lifeless body of his beautiful daughter Maud in the south side of the choir in his priory at Dunmow. Maud had been killed by a deadly poison, and her father was certain that the murderer had been sent by King John. Fitz-Walter believed he had saved his daughter when he thwarted the lecherous king's efforts to seduce her to become one of his concubines in the palace, as he had done with wives and daughters of other barons. Now, he realized, he had condemned Maud. The vengeful king had spitefully retaliated. Maud's abuse by King John and her tragic death inspired romantic stories. Poor Maud became Maid Marian in the tale of Robin Hood.[1]

Baron Fitz-Walter had been loyal to the king and had refused to join the swelling numbers of mighty barons who were planning rebellion against their sovereign. Now, overwhelmed with grief and enraged at King John, he realized John was a dangerous tyrant who had to be controlled. He became the unrelenting foe of the king and the leader of the barons' rebellion. The barons named him marshal of the Army of God and the Holy Church.

The barons were joined by the Church and the cities and towns in protesting the king's abuses against them. Their grievances were many. John had abandoned the traditional practices that his father, Henry II, and the kings who preceded him had followed, which recognized the autonomy of the Church, the privileges of the cities, and the ancient Saxon law and traditions regarding the rights of noblemen and free men.

Instead, John had arbitrarily seized Church lands and the lands and castles of his nobles. He had taken heavy tribute from the towns and merchants. He wasted this treasure on his repeatedly unsuccessful wars against France. For his abuses against the Church Pope Innocent III excommunicated John.

If anything, John was shrewd. He recognized that his loss of the Church's protection technically gave any Catholic king a claim to his crown. He made peace with the pope by transferring the sovereignty of England to Innocent III and swearing allegiance to the pope as his vassal.[2] This act alarmed the barons. They feared John's new alliance with Rome would weaken their efforts at reform unless they acted swiftly. Fitz-Walter led thousands of the barons' soldiers into the field against their king. As standard-bearer of the city of London and champion of the city leaders' grievances against King John, Fitz-Walter and his forces were welcomed through open gates into the city of London. They held control of London during the entire confrontation with John, who kept court at Windsor Castle.

Initially, John responded with fury, commanding his barons to withdraw and give sureties for their peaceful behavior and allegiance to his rule. He was a realist, however. Unable to subdue the barons because of the depleted state of his army after his most recent defeat in France, he compromised and offered to consider their grievances.

Fitz-Walter chose to present them on the open meadow of Runnymede where, protected by the Thames behind the barons and their forces and by marshes on either side, he felt secure against an ambush by the wily and desperate king. After negotiations between the barons and King John, with Stephen Langdon, archbishop of Canterbury, playing the role of mediator, a final set of promises by the king was agreed upon. John was encamped in his royal tent at Runnymede with his loyal troops surrounding him. The barons' superior number of armed infantry and cavalry occupied the greater part of the meadow, their masters' coats of arms emblazoned on a sweep of flying pennants. In this setting, the king put his royal seal to the Magna Carta.

What promises did John make in the Magna Carta? Many of the numerous provisions in the body of the charter are concerned with the ancient laws and privileges of the nobles in archaic terms that later were to become irrelevant to English law. A modern reader today would find it difficult to understand them, let alone be inspired by them. A good example is Chapter 2, in which King John promises the following:

> If any of our earls or barons, or other holding of us in chief by knight's service shall have died, and when he has died his heir shall be of full age and owe relief, he shall have his inheritance by the ancient relief; that is to say, the heir or heirs of an earl for the whole barony of an earl a hundred pounds; the heir or heirs of a baron for the whole barony a hundred pounds, the heir or heirs of a knight for a whole knight's fee a hundred shillings at most; and who owes less let him give less according to the ancient custom of fees.

This assurance that after the death of a nobleman an heir would inherit his title for the payment of a reasonable fee was based on ancient Saxon law. Obviously King John was either confiscating titles after the death of the holder or exacting exorbitant ransom for their transfer. Most of the other promises in the charter reflect in this way the king's abuses. They indicate that John had allowed his sheriffs and constables to abuse subjects and exact unlawful tributes. They also evidence the barons' outrage against John's appointment of corrupt judges, seizure and imprisonment of nobles contrary to established law, and confiscation of their property in violation of the laws that had earlier prevailed in England. Basically, King John in the charter promises not to do this anymore.

Consequently, the Magna Carta did not represent the original source of the rights it contained. It was a restatement of rights going back to the good Saxon times. Sir Edward Coke, the seventeenth-century champion of the common law of England, argued that the great charter King John was forced to accept reflected the immemorial customs and laws of England from at least the time of King Edward the Confessor, the only English king to be sainted by the Catholic Church.

Coke claimed that the Norman Conquest of 1066 c.e. did not disrupt this ancient heritage of Saxon law. Instead, he said, the conqueror William I incorporated and applied this Saxon law tradition, which blended with the Norman feudal law to become the common law of England. Henry I, a successor of William, restated this Saxon law tradition in his coronation oath, and promised to rule by it. He said, "I restore to you the law of King Edward with all the reforms which my father introduced with the consent of the barons."[3] His declaration did not achieve the fame of the Magna Carta, however. It appears to have been received by his nobles as nothing new, but rather something expected from the sovereign. King John's father, Henry II, ruled under this same tradition.

It was King John's ruthless violations of the ancient Saxon customs that roused the barons and led them to want to reenshrine the rights and liberties from King Edward the Confessor's time. The papal nuncio Pandulf cried against King John, "You are not worthy to be compared to St. Edward, you relish and enforce the evil laws of William the Bastard, and you despise the best laws of St. Edward as if they were worthless."[4] A copy of Henry I's coronation oath was brought to Runnymede by the barons and formed a basis for some of the provisions in the Magna Carta.

The one chapter in the Magna Carta that may deserve the tribute tradition has given to the charter as a whole is Chapter 39. It declares:

"No free man shall be taken, imprisoned, disseised, outlawed, banished, or in any way destroyed, nor will we proceed against or prosecute him, except by the lawful judgment of his peers and by the law of the land." Although we should not read too much of our present constitutional guarantees into this thirteenth-century provision, its words resonate familiar concepts of justice. Chapter 39 appears to be the very first declaration in a charter accepted by a ruler of the individual's right to "due process of law," which was held to be synonymous with "the law of the land" in Chapter 39 of the Magna Carta. The Fifth and Fourteenth Amendments to the U.S. Constitution use language similar to this provision in the Magna Carta when they guarantee that "no person shall be deprived of life, liberty, or property without due process of law." Even so, neither Chapter 39 nor any other provision of the Magna Carta protected the privacy of the home from unreasonable government search and seizure.

The barons well knew that King John agreed to the Magna Carta only under coercion of force. They believed he would reject his promises once free of this coercion. The barons were proved right in their assessment of John's commitment. Despite his sworn promises, after the ceremony at Runnymede King John hastened to free himself of these commitments to the barons. He protested to Pope Innocent III that he had been forced against his sovereign will by his rebellious barons to surrender his divine right to rule. The pope's outraged response was swift. Innocent III immediately issued the Papal Bull of 24 August 1215—*Etsi carissimus*—which declared:

> John our dearest son, though he had grievously offended God and the Church, has yet repented and become our vassal, and has taken the cross. But the enemy of the human race [the devil] stirred against him the barons of England—who conspiring as vassals against their lord, dared to make war on him, even seizing the city of London, the capital of the kingdom— and by such violence John was forced to accept an agreement that was shameful, illegal, and unjust, impairing his royal right and dignity. Therefore . . . we utterly reject and condemn this settlement, ordering under threat of excommunication that

> the king should not dare to observe it nor the barons require it
> to be observed, and we declare the charter, with all undertak-
> ings arising from it, to be null and void for ever.[5]

Furious at this betrayal by the king, many of the barons took up arms against him once more. Robert Fitz-Walter negotiated with Prince Louis, the son of the king of France, to come to England to be crowned king in place of John. For these acts Fitz-Walter and a number of the barons were excommunicated by the pope. However, this new rebellion was interrupted by the deaths of Pope Innocent III in July 1216 and of King John three months later. John's heir to the throne, his eldest son, Henry, was only ten years old. On being crowned Henry III, the young king ruled under the supervision of the aged earl of Pembroke, who was appointed protector of the realm.

Pembroke succeeded in routing Prince Louis and the French army that had invaded England and in arresting many of the rebellious barons, including Fitz-Walter. However, to end the strife between the barons and the throne, Pembroke and the pope's legate had young King Henry confirm the principal provisions of the Magna Carta and reissue the charter in 1225. At the same time, Henry granted a general amnesty to the barons.

When Baron Fitz-Walter was released on King Henry's amnesty, he assumed the cross to join the Crusade in Palestine. After taking part in the famous siege of Damietta, he returned home and died peacefully in 1234. He was buried near Maud in Dunmow Priory.

As a strategy to keep the peace with their nobles during the next hundred years or so, English monarchs reconfirmed the Magna Carta forty-four more times during the reigns of Edward III, Richard II, Henry IV, and Henry V. Then it became dormant for the next two hundred years until it was revived again in the early part of the seventeenth century.

From this time forward, the Magna Carta became revered in English and American history of individual rights and liberties as the law of laws, a hallowed foundation for the protection of the people against government abuse and the source of individual rights in English and American law. In reality it was none of these. Certainly, as we have seen, it is not the source of the protection in the American Bill of Rights against unreasonable searches and seizures. Nowhere in the Magna Carta are there any limitations on King John's power of search and seizure. Then why tell the story of the Magna Carta here? Because legend and tradition require it. Regardless of the actual and historical language of the charter King John accepted at Runnymede, the Magna Carta has come down to us through history in legendary form as a great charter of individual rights and liberty which influenced American and English constitutional freedom. As we shall see, we cannot ignore the legend.

The revival and, in fact, reinvention of the Magna Carta that occurred in the early part of the seventeenth century was the work of common law lawyers like Sir Edward Coke, Thomas Hedley, and John Seldon. They reached back to this storied charter of restrictions against the power of the king to challenge the assertions of absolute monarchy by James I and Charles I. In opposing these autocratic kings, they repeatedly relied on the Magna Carta for their authority, whether the actual provisions of the Magna Carta supported their arguments or not.

Coke was particularly influential in this regard. His legal opinions on the common law and the Magna Carta were especially persuasive because he straddled two worlds—that of scholarship and that of the bench, bar, and legislature. Coke had served as Queen Elizabeth's attorney general; as chief justice of the Court of Common Pleas by appointment of James I, and, off and on, as a member of the House of Commons. At the same time he held these positions, Coke was writing his *Institutes on the Common Law*, which were respected as the most scholarly and definitive statements of the law by later common law commentators and by English and American lawyers of Coke's time and later.

Oddly, while Coke as a scholar condemned in his writings general dragnet search warrants as violating the Magna Carta, he was silent on this subject as lawyer, judge, and legislator. In his *Institutes on the Common Law*, relying on the Magna Carta, he wrote:

> For a man's home is his castle . . . for where shall a man be safe if it is not in his house? . . . For though commonly the houses or cottages of poor and base people be by such [general] warrants searched, etc. yet if it be lawful; the houses of any subject, be he never so great, may be searched, etc. by such warrant upon bare surmise.[6]

In fact, there was no protection in England at this time against the king's authorization of arbitrary and dragnet searches and seizures of the homes and shops of his subjects. In search of revenues, English kings commissioned private trade and craft guilds to control their individual jurisdictions as monopolies. The king's charters authorized the guilds to conduct general searches of homes, shops, and ships to seize and forfeit unauthorized or smuggled goods or pirated publications in avoidance of license fees and taxes.[7]

As a judge and later as a member of Commons, Coke had opportunities to challenge the king's use of arbitrary search powers. He could have given practical application to his scholarly but erroneous pronouncement that general warrants not based on probable cause or specifying particular persons or places to be searched were in violation of Magna Carta. Coke, however, remained silent on this issue.

When Henry VIII broke with Rome after the pope refused to annul his marriage with Queen Catherine of Aragon, he created his own Church of England and made the Crown supreme over religious and temporal matters in the kingdom. In this rapid transformation from the Catholic Church to Henry's Episcopal Church of England, the king demanded from his subjects absolute loyalty to the principles and practices of the new faith. Any failure to switch devotion to the new church was declared by statute and the king's edict to be heresy and treason.

A submissive Parliament enacted statutes during Henry's, and later Elizabeth I's, reigns recognizing the supremacy of the Crown over the

Church of England and authorizing the creation of the Crown's High Commission.[8] The commission was granted unlimited power to protect the kingdom from "[a]ll manner of error, heresies, schisms, abuses, offenses, contempts, and enormities."[9]

The members of the High Commission sat as an ecclesiastic court of inquisition, compelling suspected violators to testify under oath on the basis of secret accusations. The commission tried these suspects without being bound by the constraints of the common law courts or by rules of evidence and other procedures to ensure fairness and objectivity under the law of the land. Also, unlike the common law courts, the commission's decisions could not be appealed.

In addition, as an investigative weapon, parliament gave the High Commission broad and general powers to authorize searches of homes, churches, and shops and the seizure of books, papers, and any other items suspected of being evidence of violations within the commission's jurisdiction. These were general warrants that did not identify particular persons, particular places, or particular things. The searchers had total discretion as to whose house to search. The High Commission made wide use of informers to assist them in raiding suspected houses. It appeared to be of no concern to the commission that many of their informers were themselves serious criminals who used their information to obtain freedom from arrest or conviction. With the presence of such informers everywhere, secret Catholics greatly feared unannounced raids on their houses and made elaborate efforts to hide any item that could connect them to their forbidden religion.[10]

As chief justice of the Court of Common Pleas, Coke challenged the power of the High Commission to fine and imprison convicted individuals. He claimed that the commission's exercise of such powers was against the law of the land, and thus in violation of the Magna Carta. He issued numerous writs of prohibition against these acts of the commission. Yet, Coke never challenged the sweeping dragnet search and seizure powers of the High Commission. When he was attorney general under

Queen Elizabeth, Coke dutifully enforced these unreasonable searches and seizures of the High Commission. His silence as chief justice on this subject may have been influenced by his former conduct.

Coke's judicial interference with the king's High Commission infuriated James I, and he summoned Coke to appear before the Privy Counsel. The debate between the king's ministers and Coke became so heated that on one occasion, in a confrontation with the king himself, Coke became so combative that he almost came to blows with His Royal Majesty. Suddenly realizing the extreme danger he was courting, Coke fell to all fours and groveled before King James. Lord Salisbury, Coke's friend, intervened and James pardoned Coke.[11]

Later, when Charles I was king, he asserted absolute power over Parliament and exercised arbitrary authority to arrest and imprison members of Commons without charge. Coke, now a member of Commons, was again silent on the subject of restricting the king's arbitrary search powers. He did, however, protest the king's unlawful imprisonment of members of Commons as being in violation of Magna Carta.

The struggle between Parliament and king over supremacy had heightened. Parliament had refused appropriations requested by the king. Charles ordered five members of Commons, who were also knights, to lend him the money withheld from him. When they refused, Charles had them arrested and thrown in prison. They sought their release on habeas corpus, but a timid court took no action.

The Five Knights case brought on a fierce confrontation between Commons and King Charles, with Coke leading the fight for Commons. Parliament gained greater confidence in its efforts when the five knights were reelected to Commons while they were in prison. Coke insisted that Charles agree to a bill of rights, which Coke drafted. It required the king to reaffirm his allegiance to Magna Carta and to agree to not arbitrarily arrest and imprison subjects without charge and without rights to bail and habeas corpus.

King Charles refused to be bound by a bill of rights enacted by Parliament. He said he would agree only to a general bill confirming the Great Charter, but "without additions, paraphrases, or explanations."[12] Coke finally agreed to draft a document less compelling than a bill. He prepared a Petition of Right, which was only a request to the king to grant it and agree to abide by it. The House of Commons and the House of Lords, after long debate among themselves and with the king, finally approved the Petition of Right and presented it to King Charles for the king's signature and seal. Under this petition, the king was asked to confirm the principles of Magna Carta and to agree not to imprison persons without charge, without bail, or without access to habeas corpus as required by Magna Carta.[13]

Charles indignantly replied that the king need not be so distrusted by his Parliament that a written agreement be imposed on him. He agreed to confirm Magna Carta and rule by its principles but insisted that Parliament should take his royal word on this, which, he claimed, was much better than a written paper. Parliament, with the leverage of withholding the appropriations Charles so badly needed, insisted on a written Petition of Right, which Charles finally signed, saying, "Let it be done as it is desired."

Despite Coke's leadership in this confrontation with the king and his authorship of the Petition of Right, there is no provision in the petition aimed at curbing the king's arbitrary and unreasonable search and seizure practices. This absence tends to call into question Coke's role as a champion against unreasonable searches and seizures in English law.

Indeed, Coke became the victim of such a search. After he retired to his country home to continue his legal writings, King Charles, worried about the political impact of Coke's writings, got the Privy Council to issue a general warrant for "seditious and dangerous papers." The messenger sent by the Privy Council to make the search ransacked Coke's house and seized not only all of Coke's books and papers, but also his will, money, jewelry, and other valuables. One account has this wanton search and seizure in Coke's home occur while Coke was lying in bed dying.[14]

Part of Coke's legacy was the transformation of the historical Magna Carta to a legendary charter of individual liberty and rights. As a judge and member of Commons, Coke repeatedly based his challenges of the king's arbitrary practices on the authority of Magna Carta—so much so that he inspired the beliefs of many lawyers of his time and of those later, particularly in colonial America, that Magna Carta was truly the source of the Englishman's individual liberty and rights.

Never mind that Coke did not in practice challenge arbitrary general search warrants that were frequently employed by the Crown and its agents. His romanticizing of the Magna Carta in so many other instances provided the charter with the aura of a sacred grant of all individual rights against abusive government, including protection against unreasonable searches and seizures. Besides, Coke did pronounce in his scholarly writings that the Magna Carta prohibited arbitrary general warrants. Coke's authoritative statements of law on general search warrants were relied upon and repeated by the great common law commentators who followed him: Blackstone, *Commentaries on the Law of England*; Hawkins, *A Treatise of the Please of the Crown*; and Hale, *The History of the Pleas of the Crown*.

In addition, all lawyers of the seventeenth and eighteenth centuries read Coke as part of their legal training and quoted him later in their cases. Even nonlawyers like John Wilkes were familiar with Coke. As we shall see, Wilkes, a radical member of Commons, challenged the general search warrant issued against him by George III's secretary of state as violating Magna Carta.

American lawyers in the colonies were also trained on Coke. In the famous Writs of Assistance case, involving the issuance of the most general of general warrants, which we will discuss later, James Otis argued against the Crown that these unreasonable search warrants were prohibited by the Magna Carta and cited Coke as his authority. A young John Adams was in the courtroom. Adams was inspired by Otis's argument and later claimed that it sparked the American Revolution.

Surely, Thomas Jefferson and James Madison had read Coke in their legal training. The legend of the ancient Magna Carta as a charter of individual liberty may have inspired their confidence in drafting the Declaration of Independence and the Bill of Rights, including the Fourth Amendment protection against unreasonable searches and seizures.

Thus, it does not matter that the actual promises King John made to the barons in 1215 would not have inspired the American Bill of Rights. If the legend and the myth were strong enough, the impact on the history of individual liberty that tradition attributes to the Magna Carta may have to be recognized. Recently, scholars have seriously done so. In a series of books published by the University of Virginia Press in 1995 in celebration of the Magna Carta, Morris Ashley wrote:

> When that historic event at Runnymede, which we are again celebrating this year, was being commemorated fifty years ago, it was said by a distinguished scholar that there had in fact been two Great Charters: the original Magna Carta conceded by King John to his barons in 1215, and the Charter as it was interpreted by the opponents or critics of the Stuart Monarchy in seventeenth-century England. These critics—lawyers for the most part—had, it was felt, elevated or transformed what was, in origin a "feudal" or "medieval" constitutional document into the palladium of English liberties.[15]

Similarly, Richard L. Perry and John C. Cooper credit the Magna Carta as a founding source in their book *Sources of Our Liberties.* Explaining the role of the Magna Carta as a source of American liberty, the authors write:

> The liberties of the American citizen depend upon the existence of established and known rules of law limiting the authority and the discretion of men wielding the power of gov-

ernment. Magna Carta announced the rule of law; this was its
great contribution. It is this characteristic which has provided
throughout the years the foundation on which has come to rest
the entire structure of Anglo-American constitutional liberties.[16]

The Petition of Right did not end the struggle between Parliament
and Charles I. Charles refused to comply with the petition. Unwilling to
negotiate any more with Charles, Parliament decided it had to remove
him as king, and the Civil War of 1642 began. Parliament's military
forces, led by Oliver Cromwell, an obscure Puritan member of Commons,
were successful in defeating the king's loyal forces. Charles was captured,
tried and convicted for treason by a special court, and beheaded.

Despite this victory, Parliament lost power instead of gaining it.
Oliver Cromwell, refusing a crown that Parliament offered, ruled
England as a dictator under a kingless protectorate. He brooked no interference from Parliament. On Cromwell's death, his son became the
Protector, but proved to be so incompetent that Cromwell's top general
invited Charles II to return to England from France to rule as king. For a
revitalized Parliament this was no solution. Charles II and James II, who
followed him to the throne, sought to restore absolute monarchy. In frus-
tration, Parliament invited Prince William of Orange and his wife, Mary,
who was James II's daughter, to come to England and rule as king and
queen. They accepted the invitation, and James fled to France, too weak
to oppose what has been called the Glorious Revolution of 1688.

King William III and Queen Mary II were required by Parliament
to swear to rule under a Bill of Rights enacted by Parliament in 1689,
which reinstated the rule of law of the Magna Carta and the supremacy
of Parliament. Once again, it is significant that there was no provision in
this Bill of Rights protecting against unreasonable searches and seizures.
In fact, Parliament itself showed its indifference to the evil of dragnet
general warrants by authorizing such sweeping intrusions into the privacy of people's homes as a strategy to enforce new tax provisions.

This time it was the new king, William III, who objected to such searches. The king got Parliament to rescind the new tax law, stating that the searches required for its enforcement constituted "a badge of slavery upon the whole people exposing every man's house to be entered into and searched by persons unknown to him."[17] As we shall see, George III, a successor to King William III, had no such qualms.

CHAPTER 2

Wilkes and Liberty

I fear neither your prosecution nor your persecution; and I will assert the security of my house, the liberty of my person, and every right of the people, not so much for my own sake, as for the sake of every one of my English fellow subjects.

John Wilkes, reply to Secretary of State Halifax,
May 9, 1763

It was not until more than one hundred years after Coke's death that the courts of England first dealt with the legality of general search warrants, which had been issued under royal authority since the Magna Carta. During the sixteenth and seventeenth centuries, neither Parliament nor the courts were focused on the Crown's use of general search warrants. Instead, their attention was drawn to the long period of strife between the king and Parliament for supremacy. George III was now king. Following a series of British monarchs who had been shorn of much of their power by Parliament, George III was determined to regain royal power. His mother had told him, "George, be king."[1]

From the beginning of George III's reign, his nemesis was a roustabout but very popular member of the House of Commons, John Wilkes. Wilkes came from a family of strict Calvinists. His mother wanted him to become a leader in this religion that shunned singing, dancing, and fun. At his mother's urging, John married the daughter of an extremely strict Calvinist family. The marriage soon bored him, and he left his new wife to join a group of carefree young men whose principal pursuits were sex, food, and drink in the filthy and stinking London of the mid-eighteenth century.

A group of anonymous writers and printers published a pamphlet called *The North Briton* in opposition to a pamphlet published by the king's ministers called *The Briton*. It was an open secret that John Wilkes was the principal writer and publisher of this pamphlet critical of the king's ministers. The king was furious over this pamphlet, which he believed published seditious libel, but forbore taking any action.[2]

All that changed with the publication of *The North Briton No. 45* on April 23, 1763.[3] George III had recently approved and signed the Treaty of Paris, which ended the Seven Years' War between England and France and Spain. The king opened the next session of Parliament with a speech from the throne, which lauded the treaty as "honorable to my crown and beneficial to my people."[4] He was more right than wrong in this boast, since by the treaty England gained extensive territory, including Canada, and won control over the Atlantic.

The North Briton No. 45 viciously attacked the speech as fraudulent and lies and claimed that the treaty was not a victory, but a defeat for England.[5] Conscious of the danger of directly attacking the king, the writer (presumably Wilkes) opened his attack on the speech with the cautionary language, "The king's speech has always been considered by the legislature and by the public at large as the speech of the minister."[6] The writer thus made it clear he was charging that the ministers themselves had insulted the king by abusing their position by putting lies into the mouth of a virtuous prince.

"Every friend of his country," the writer wrote, "must lament that a prince of so many great and amiable qualities, whom England truly reveres, can be brought to give the sanction of his sacred name to the most odious measure and to the must unjustifiable public declarations, from a throne ever renowned for truth, honor, and unsullied virtue."[7] *North Briton No. 45* then charged that the king's ministers had betrayed

England's Prussian ally and had given back to the French and Spanish most of what England had conquered. It stated that the negotiations of the king's ministers were such as to have "drawn the contempt of mankind on our wretched negotiators. . . . It is, however, remarkable that the minister's speech dwells on the *entire approbation of Parliament* to [the negotiations] which I venture to say, he must by this time be ashamed of. . . by which such immense advantages both of trade and territory were sacrificed to our inveterate enemies."[8]

Despite the writer's effort to focus his criticism on the king's ministers, and not on the king, the king was personally enraged over this publication and wanted the writers, printers, and publishers punished for seditious libel. On April 30, 1763, the secretary of state, the Earl of Halifax, issued a general warrant to the secretary's messengers "[t]o make strict and diligent search for the authors, printers, and publishers of a seditious and treasonable paper entitled the *North Briton Number 45* . . . and them or any of them having found to apprehend and seize together with their papers and to bring in safe custody before me to be examined concerning the premises and further dealt with according to law."[9]

This warrant is noteworthy in that it did not specifically name any person as an author, printer, or publisher but left it to the complete discretion of the messengers to act on rumor or sheer hunch as to whose house they would break into and search.[10] As a member of the House of Commons, Wilkes had earlier denounced a general warrant as illegal and in violation of the Magna Carta.[11] When the messengers came to his door, he told them they had an unlawful warrant and he would resist it. Halifax's messengers forced their way into Wilkes's house, ransacked it, and seized all his books and papers and other private property. They seized Wilkes and took him before Halifax, who committed him to the Tower to await trial.[12]

Later, Wilkes described this violent search of his house and the seizure of his person to the House of Commons:

On the 30th of April, in the morning, I was made a prisoner in
my own house, by some of the king's messengers. I demanded
by what authority they had forced themselves into my room,
and was shown a warrant which no person was named in particular, but generally the authors, printers, and publishers of a
seditious and treasonable paper, entitled the *North Briton, No.
45.* The messengers insisted on my going before Lord Halifax,
which I absolutely refused, because the warrant was, I thought,
illegal, and did not respect me. I was afterward carried by violence before the earls of Egrement and Halifax . . . and hurried
away to the Tower by another warrant. . . . I was detained as a
close prisoner and no person was suffered to come near me for
almost three days, although my counsel and several of my
friends demanded admittance in order to concert the means of
recovering my liberty. My house was plundered, my bureaus
broken open . . . and all my papers carried away.[13]

The news of Wilkes's noisy protest of his arrest and search of his
house spread widely through London. He was hailed by the citizens of
London, particularly the merchants, as a courageous defender of the
rights of Englishmen. Huge numbers of his supporters demonstrated in
the streets shouting out their new cry: "Wilkes and Liberty!"[14] Wilkes was
brought to the Court of Common Pleas before Chief Justice John Pratt.
Pratt ignored the issue of the general warrant's validity and discharged
Wilkes on the ground that as a member of Commons, Wilkes was privi-
leged from being arrested and charged.[15]

Pandemonium broke loose in the streets of London. Repeating the
cry, "Wilkes and Liberty," hundreds of citizens paraded in celebration of
Wilkes's victory over King George.[16] On gaining his freedom, Wilkes sent
the secretaries of state a letter on May 6, 1763:

My Lords,

On my return here from Westminster Hall, where I have been
discharged from my commitment to the Tower under your
lordships warrant, I find that my house has been robbed and
am informed that the stolen goods are in the possession of one

or both of your lordships. I therefore insist that you do forth-
with return them to Your humble servant John Wilkes[17]

The secretaries of state replied the next day, May 7, 1763:

SIR,

In answer to your letter of yesterday, in which you take upon
yourself to make use of indecent and scurrilous expressions of
your having "found your house had been robbed" and that "the
stolen goods are in our possession": we acquaint you that your
papers were seized in consequence of a heavy charge brought
against you, for being the author of an infamous and seditious
libel, tending to inflame the mind, and alienate the affections
of the people from his majesty, and excite them to traitorous
insurrections against the government; for which libel, notwith-
standing your discharge from your commitment to the Tower,
his majesty has ordered you to be prosecuted by his attorney
general.

We are at a loss to guess what you mean by "stolen goods": but
such of your papers as do not lead to proof of your guilt, shall
be restored to you; such as are necessary for that purpose, it was
our duty to deliver over to those, whose office it is to collect
the evidence, and manage the prosecution against you.

We are Your humble servants, Egremont Dunk Halifax[18]

Wilkes and the printers, whose houses had been ransacked under
the general warrant issued by Secretary of State Halifax, sued Halifax and
his messengers for civil damages. In each case, the jury found against
Halifax and awarded substantial damages. Wilkes received the highest
award, £1,000 against the messenger and £4,000 against the secretary of
state.[19]

On appeal, the cases came before Chief Justice John Pratt, now ele-
vated to a peerage as Lord Camden. Lord Camden upheld the jury verdicts
and awards in all cases. His strongest opinion, declaring the general warrant issued by Halifax unlawful, was in the case of *Entick v. Carrington.*[20]

Entick was one of the printers subjected to the dragnet search, and Carrington was one of Halifax's messengers who made the search.

This case led William Pitt to make his famous statement in Parliament that no matter how poor a man's hovel is, even if the rain and wind could come in, the king of England could not enter. According to Pitt, his friend, Lord Camden, had reaffirmed the Magna Carta and the principle that a man's home is his castle. The news of Lord Camden's opinion and Pitt's interpretation reached the American colonies as fast as a sailing ship could bring it. At that time, the colonists were being subjected to arbitrary general warrants and the even broader writs of assistance, which permitted the king's agents to enter and search at random their shops and homes, particularly to enforce the hated excise taxes.

To the colonists, Lord Camden's opinion in *Entick v. Carrington* became the benchmark for the rights of Englishmen, which, they bitterly complained, they were being denied, particularly in the enforcement of excise taxes. Pitt and the colonists, however, were wrong. Lord Camden had not struck a blow against the king's power, although his rhetoric sounded as though he had. His decision was limited to holding that the secretary of state lacked jurisdiction to issue general warrants. Halifax had defended his warrant on the ground of earlier practice and precedent by former secretaries of state. But Lord Camden held that a tradition of unlawful practice will not transform the practice into a lawful one. He suggested that the earlier secretaries of state may have gotten away with it because the judges at that time were too timid to challenge the practice.[21]

However, Lord Camden's opinion clearly said that the king in council certainly had the power to issue general warrants. He distinguished certain cases from Entick's where these warrants had been upheld by the courts as valid on the ground that the *king had commanded it*.[22] True it is that Lord Camden's condemnation of general warrants issued by the secretary of state was written in stirring language. Speaking of the issuing of general warrants by secretaries of state, Lord Camden declared, "It is high time to put an end to them."²³ Lord Camden distinguished between publishing a libel and keeping it privately in one's desk at home. He ruled that the secretary of state could not "lawfully break in to a man's house and study to search for evidence against him; this would be worse than the Spanish Inquisition; for ransacking a man's secret drawers and Boxes to come at evidence against him, is like racking his body to come at his secret thoughts. . . . This would be monstrous, indeed; and if it were lawful, no man could endure to live in this country."²⁴

Stirring as these words were, they were qualified by the court's acknowledgment that the king himself had this awesome power. Thus, the outrage the colonists felt at being treated unequally with Englishmen at home, which helped to spark the American Revolution, was a providential misunderstanding of Lord Camden's ruling on general warrants.

That ruling, however, was tremendously popular in England, especially since it further vindicated the people's hero, John Wilkes. Lord Camden became a hero figure to the people. He was greeted joyously in the streets of London and was deferred to with great honor and respect at public events and places. An industry developed in the reproduction of his portrait, which was hung on large boards outside public inns and alehouses.²⁵ This popularity did not endear Lord Camden to the king and his ministers.

The court victory made Wilkes cocky and defiant. He wanted to tweak the king's nose again. Over the strong objections of his friends and closest advisors, Wilkes decided to republish *North Briton No. 45*. He did so openly on his own press, and the king's attorney general lost no time in charging him again with seditious libel. In addition, he was charged with obscenity because, in the original search of his house, the messengers had found copies of an indecent poem called *Essay on Women*, which Wilkes had printed but claimed he had no intention of distributing.²⁶

It was obvious that Wilkes was counting on the court discharging him again because of his privilege as a member of Parliament. But the king outmaneuvered Wilkes by pressuring Commons to revoke the privilege in Wilkes's case. The obscenity charge against Wilkes caused him to lose many of his supporters in Commons, who voted overwhelmingly to revoke his privilege.[27] Wilkes was now vulnerable to be tried on the king's charges against him.

In addition, an enemy of Wilkes picked a fight with him, and in the ensuing duel, Wilkes was wounded in the thigh.[28] When he had sufficiently recovered to travel, Wilkes quietly went to Paris to recuperate at his daughter's home there. In Paris, he resorted to his usual excesses in sex and food and became too ill to return to London to attend the next session of Commons. He wrote to the Speaker explaining his illness and providing supporting statements of his attending physician. He asked for a brief continuance to appear in Commons, but the Speaker denied this request on the technical ground that it had not been properly certified. Accordingly, as punishment, Wilkes was expelled from the House of Commons.[29]

A further disaster for Wilkes occurred when his trial in the Court of King's Bench was held while he was absent in France. The court found Wilkes guilty on the charges but withheld sentence until Wilkes was back in the country. However, the court entered a sentence of outlawry against Wilkes for his failure to appear in the court, when commanded, for trial. As an outlaw, Wilkes was in great danger, since that status took away his citizenship and rights under the law.[30] Theoretically, he could be killed on sight. It would be essential for him to have his outlawry revoked.

Despite these perils, Wilkes returned to England openly and immediately drew attention to himself by entering the election for a London seat in the House of Commons. He was roundly trounced. His spirit undampened, Wilkes turned around and successfully ran for a seat from the County of Middlesex. His bold plan and his success in carrying it out renewed his popularity among the ordinary citizens and merchants. Once again, large crowds hailed him in public and took up the cry of "Wilkes and Liberty."[31]

Wilkes now wanted to challenge his sentence of outlawry and appeared in court with his lawyer before Lord Mansfield. Fully aware of how much trouble Wilkes had been in earlier proceedings, Mansfield did not want to go forward and ruled that Wilkes was not lawfully before him because he had not been arrested. Wilkes contacted the sheriff and requested to be arrested, which he was. Brought into court under arrest, Wilkes was now entitled to a hearing by Mansfield. The issue first presented before the court was the validity of the sentence of outlawry. Angry crowds of Wilkes's supporters had threatened Mansfield and jostled him on the street when he was going to the court.[32]

This led Mansfield to make one of the most boastful judicial statements in history on the independence and objectivity of the judiciary. Mansfield paused in his review of the case to address the courtroom. He said he had received many anonymous letters, some of them threatening, pressuring him to reverse the outlawry. He said he had been told that consequences of a frightful nature would flow from the establishing of the outlawry; that people wouldn't endure an unfavorable decision against Wilkes and would resist it. Mansfield responded to these pressures, saying,

> These are arguments which will not weigh a feather with me. . . . He must be a weak man, indeed who can be staggered by such a consideration. . . . Those who imagine judges are capable of being influenced by such unworthy, indirect means, most grossly deceive themselves; and for my own part, I trust that my temper, and the color and conduct of my life, have clothed me with a suit of armor to shield me from such arrows. . . . If I have discharged my duty as a public or private character, by endeavoring to preserve pure and perfect the principles of the constitution, maintain unsullied the honor of the courts of justice, and, by an upright administration of, to give a due effect to the laws, I have hitherto done it without any other gift or reward than that most pleasing and most honorable one, the conscientious conviction of doing what was right.[33]

Despite this expression of righteous courage, Mansfield never-theless reversed the outlawry on a most technical and specious ground. Mansfield ruled that the proceedings were erroneously stated as *at the County Court for the County of Middlesex*, when they should have been stated as *at the County Court of Middlesex for the County of Middlesex*.[34] Such a distinction without a difference convinced the crowds, both inside and outside the courtroom, that Mansfield had indeed been too frightened to rule against Wilkes.

Of course, it now remained for Mansfield to sentence Wilkes on his convictions of sedition and obscenity. By then, Lord Camden had ruled that the secretary of state had no power or jurisdiction to issue his gen-eral warrant. All of the evidence the prosecution produced at Wilkes's trial to obtain the guilty verdicts had been the fruit of this unlawful search. The unlawfulness of the search was sufficient to justify heavy damages against Halifax and his agents. Why, then, could this same ille-gally seized evidence support Wilkes's conviction and justify a sentence of punishment?

This is a disturbing question we will return to later. Suffice it to say that neither Wilkes nor his lawyer objected to the convictions on this ground. They would not even have thought of such an objection, since English law permitted the use of illegally seized evidence so long as it was relevant and reliable. This was so even if the lawless officials involved were liable for damages. Wilkes was sentenced to twenty-two months in prison.[35]

CHAPTER 3

A Flame of Fire

If the king of Great Britain in person were encamped on Boston Common at the head of twenty thousand men, with all his navy on our coast, he would not be able to execute these laws. They would be resisted or eluded.

James Otis, in arguing in the Council Chamber of the Old Town House in Boston,
against the writs of assistance,
February 1761

The Treaty of Paris gave England control over Canada, which, together with the British colonies in America, offered the mother country a unique opportunity for monopolistic trade. George III was determined to take advantage of this opportunity and to enforce his trade laws strictly. The colonists were not hostile to these trade laws, as such, because they recognized their obligation, as English subjects, to assist their country economically. However, they refused to tolerate the enforcement of the trade laws through writs of assistance and the imposition by Parliament of excise taxes on specific products, such as cider, to be enforced by writs of assistance.

A writ of assistance was the broadest and vaguest of all general warrants. The holder of such a writ had unlimited authority to enter any home, shop, ship, or warehouse, at his discretion, to search broadly for contraband or evidence of violation of the tax laws. Worse yet, the writ of assistance gave the holder the right to command the assistance of others to provide the manpower for sweeping dragnet searches.[1]

In addition, the colonists bitterly objected to Parliament's exercise of authority to tax them. The colonies had no representation in Parliament, and they claimed that English law and tradition, going back to the Magna Carta, required the assent of the people to taxes through their elected representatives in Parliament. "No taxation without representation" became the cry of the protesting colonists, a cry that grew angrier, finally bursting into a major cause for rebellion.

The writs of assistance, however, were the yoke the colonists would not bear. They saw the writs as a stamp of second-class citizenship because they believed their fellow citizens in England suffered no such abuse. The issue came to a head in 1760 when the chief of customs in Boston requested the Superior Court of Boston to renew his authority to issue writs of assistance after the death of King George II. Chief Justice Stephen Sewall, publicly respected for his integrity and moderation, expressed grave doubts over the court's authority to issue such writs. Nevertheless, because the petition was on behalf of the Crown, he ordered a hearing at which the opposing parties would present their arguments to the court.[2]

The officers of customs asked James Otis, then advocate general for the admiralty, to argue the Crown's case in support of the writs of assistance. Otis refused, stating he so strongly opposed writs of assistance he would not prostitute his office to the support of an oppressive act. He resigned as advocate general, and, with the assistance of a colleague, Oxenbridge Thatcher, agreed to represent the Boston merchants against the petition for writs of assistance.[3]

There may be another explanation for Otis's resignation and taking on the other side. The position of chief justice of the court had been promised by William Shirley, the previous governor, to Otis's father, Colonel James Otis, a revered and successful Boston lawyer, when a vacancy occurred. Young Otis asked Lieutenant Governor Thomas Hutchinson, a close friend of his father, to help his father get the appointment. Instead, however, when Chief Justice Sewall died, at the outset of the Writs of Assistance case, Hutchinson took the appointment as chief justice for himself from the new governor, recently arrived from England. In addition to not being a lawyer, Hutchinson was a politician and chose to continue to keep the political positions he held, in addition to being chief justice. Thus, Hutchinson was at the same time lieutenant governor, a member of the legislative council, judge of probate, and chief justice of the Massachusetts Supreme Court.[4]

There can be no doubt that James Otis was outraged over this betrayal of his father. He may well have been so furious with the government that his resignation as advocate general and acceptance of the cause of the merchants could have resulted from a desire for revenge. Indeed, at the time, it was reported that Otis had said that he would set the province in flames, though he perished in the fire.[5] When some officials ascribed this base motive to Otis and accused him of having no patriotism, John Adams, later to be president, rejected this calumny and asked why James Otis would be upset over his father's not getting a job that paid so much less than he earned in his law practice.[6]

The potential for high drama became strong when the Crown chose Jeremiah Gridley to argue its case for the writs of assistance. Gridley had taught both Otis and Thatcher in the law.[7] Master and students would be on opposite sides in this critical case, called Paxton's Case after the name of the head of customs.

The only knowledge we have of Otis's argument that day comes from the notes John Adams took in the courtroom and from a letter he wrote to a friend fifty-six years later on March 29, 1817. John Adams had not yet been admitted to the bar when the argument occurred. He rode to Boston with Samuel Quincy, also a neophyte lawyer, to attend the argument under special dispensation of the court. Adams was inspired by Otis's presentation, finding in it the fundamental basis for colonial freedom and revolution. In his recollection of the event to his friend William

Tudor in 1817, Adams exclaimed

> The scene is the Council Chamber in the Old Town House in Boston. . . . Otis was a flame of fire! . . . with a promptitude of classic allusions, a depth of research, a rapid summary of historical events and dates, a profusion of legal authorities, a prophetic glance of his eye into futurity, and a torrent of impetuous elegance. He hurried away everything before him. American independence was then and there born; the seeds of patriots and heroes were then and there sown, to defend vigorous youth. . . . Every man of a crowded audience appeared to me to go away, as I did, ready to take arms against Writs of Assistance. Then and there was the first scene of the first act of opposition to the arbitrary claims of Great Britain. In fifteen years, namely in 1776, he grew up to manhood and declared himself free.[8]

After the arguments that day, Chief Justice Hutchinson announced that he would delay a decision until he received more advice from London. In time he received a copy of an authorized writ of assistance used in London and gave it to the Crown prosecutor, Gridley, to use against Otis. Gridley argued in renewed proceedings that "If it is law in England, it is law here."[9] Otis still protested that such a general writ was against the Magna Carta and the constitution of England. However Hutchinson decided for the Crown and granted a new writ of assistance.[10]

An odd sequence of events kept the lives of Otis and Hutchinson entangled. Hutchinson blamed Otis when an angry mob later wrecked his mansion and forced him to flee with his family in August 1765. Otis himself went from acclaimed hero to destitute alcoholic. Hutchinson presided over the examining board, which proclaimed the ravaged Otis "a distracted or lunatic person." Otis was shipped, bound, to an isolated farm in Nantasket, Massachusetts, where he was killed at the age of fifty-eight in 1783 by a thunderbolt that struck the farmhouse.[11] Ironically, after Hutchinson escaped to England from the Revolution, his restored mansion became the home of Otis's sister, Mercy Otis Warren.[12]

Looking back from the vantage point of 1817, former president John Adams observed that unreasonable searches and seizures by British officers helped spark the Revolution. In 1776, having freed itself from England, the new nation now could write its own laws, basing them on the liberty rights of the individual citizen, which symbolized and were the foundation of the Revolution.

Yet the new Constitution of the United States, drafted by the Constitutional Convention and approved by Congress, provided no explicit protection against unreasonable searches and seizures.[13] Indeed, it contained no Bill of Rights at all to protect individual citizens from government tyranny. When, during the convention, delegates like George Mason of Virginia urged the inclusion of a Bill of Rights, the opponents in the majority replied that a democracy governed by the people through elected representatives needed no Bill of Rights. Such documents through history were only necessary to protect the people from the abuses of power of kings by specific restrictions on those powers.

Furthermore, the opponents argued that the federal Congress under the Constitution is only given specific and limited powers, none of which would permit them to invade any of the natural, inalienable rights of the citizens. Thus, why prohibit what Congress has no power to do? Providing such a list of protections would be seen by some as weakening the limitations on the Congress. The existence of such restrictions on Congress some would argue must mean that Congress had the power, from the beginning, to engage in that conduct.

A further danger they pointed to was that it was impossible to draft a list of all the natural rights of a citizen, and the need to include some, but not others, would be interpreted as a determination that those excluded were not fundamental individual rights. Also, the opponents stressed that the Constitution reserved to the states and the people all powers not specifically given to the federal government. Thus, the people would be protected by state bills of rights.[14]

During the ratification process in the states, however, many people balked at agreeing to a charter of government without a Bill of Rights. They had only recently been under the yoke of King George III and had fought the Revolution to once and for all time have these basic individual rights guaranteed to them. In addition, their leaders scoffed at the argument of the convention delegates that Congress was given no power to revoke any of these rights. They pointed to the clause following the specification of congressional authority, which permitted Congress to do everything "necessary and proper" to carry out its powers. There, these state leaders declared, was the large hole in the argument of the constitutional limitations of the powers of the Congress.[15]

Although the Constitution was ratified by the states without a Bill of Rights, it clearly was on the assumption that the first Congress would reconsider the issue of a Bill of Rights through amendments to the Constitution.[16] James Madison emphasized in the first Congress that so many citizens had opposed the Constitution because of the absence of a Bill of Rights that it was necessary to provide such a guarantee of rights if the new federal government was to obtain the support and confidence of the people.[17]

A particular mystery in the Constitution that was ratified by the states is the failure of the delegates to include a provision against unreasonable searches and seizures in one of the articles of the Constitution. If, as we have seen, unreasonable searches and seizures were partly responsible for igniting the Revolution, it would be logical to assume that protection against such invasions of privacy would be given prominent attention in the new Constitution. For the same reasons the inclusion of a Bill of Rights was rejected, the majority of the delegates probably believed that a free democracy based on the will of the people had no reason to fear unreasonable searches and seizures by government officials.

But why, then, did the delegates think it necessary to protect the right to habeas corpus in Article I, Section 9 (2), the rights against bills of attainder and ex post facto laws in Article I, Section 9 (3), and the right to a jury trial in criminal cases in Article III, Section 2 (3)? Nothing in the debates in the convention or during the ratification of the Constitution by the states provides any explanation. The danger of just selecting these rights to include in the Constitution was expressed by one of the delegates, Robert Whitehill, as follows:

> I wish it to be seriously considered whether we have a right to leave the liberties of the people to such future constructions and expositions as may possibly be made upon this system; particularly when its advocates, even at this day confess that it would be dangerous to omit anything in the enumeration of a bill of rights, and according to this principle, the reservations of the habeas corpus, and trial by jury in criminal cases, may hereafter be construed to be the only privileges reserved for the people.[18]

Perhaps the closest insight to this omission of other rights in the Constitution is supplied by Governor Edmund Randolph in his statements against a Bill of Rights during the debate on the Constitution in the Virginia Convention in 1788. Reaching the issue of the need for a bill of rights protection against unreasonable searches and seizures, Randolph said:

> That general warrants are grievous and oppressive, and ought not to be granted, I fully admit. I heartily concur expressing my detestation of them. But we have sufficient security here also. We do not rely on the integrity of one particular person or body; but on the number and different orders of the members of the government. Some of them having necessarily the same feelings with ourselves. Can it be believed that the federal judiciary would not be independent enough to prevent such aggressive practices? If they will not do justice to persons injured, may they not go to our own state judiciaries and obtain it?[19]

Indeed, by the time of the ratification of the Constitution, every state had a Bill of Rights, except New Jersey, which had a provision protecting against general warrants. The first such declaration was in the Virginia Bill of Rights of 1776. Drafted by George Mason, the Virginia search and seizure provision condemned general warrants and stated that all warrants issued without evidence and calling for seizure of persons not named or things not particularly described are "grievous and oppressive and ought not to be granted."[20]

Most other states generally copied this provision from the Virginia Bill of Rights. However, Massachusetts's Declaration of Rights of 1780 was the first to use the phrase "unreasonable searches and seizures"[21] and became a model for the Fourth Amendment.[22] It was clear, however, in each of the state provisions that the prohibited searches and seizures were those made under general warrants.

Despite the ratification of the Constitution, the strong opposition to the absence of a Bill of Rights in the document led Congress to agree to initiate amendments to establish a Bill of Rights. The amendment that sought to prohibit general warrants and writs of assistance is the fourth, which declares in its finally approved form:

> The right of the people to be secure in their persons, houses, papers, and effects against unreasonable searches and seizures, shall not be violated, and no warrant shall issue, but upon probable cause, supported by oath or affirmation, and particularly describing the place to be searched, and the persons or things to be seized.

But this form of wording of the Fourth Amendment was not the one approved by the House of Representatives, which had formed itself into a Committee of the Whole to review the Bill of Rights amendments. Indeed, the committee had rejected this form.[23] The committee had favored, instead, Madison's wording, modeled on the Massachusetts Declaration of Rights:

> *The right of the people to be secure in their persons, houses, papers, and effects, shall not be violated by warrants issuing without*

*probable cause, supported by oath or affirmation, and not particu-
larly describing the place to be searched, and the persons or things to
be seized.*[24]

After approving this language, the committee sent the amendment
to a small committee on style, chaired by delegate Egbert Benson, whose
amendment to change Madison's wording had been rejected by the committee. Benson reported back the wording of his failed amendment, and
no one seems to have noticed.[25] It was Benson's version that was
approved and that ultimately became the Fourth Amendment.[26]

This oversight on the part of the House did not affect the validity
of the Fourth Amendment as finally approved by Congress and ratified
by the states, but it created ambiguity and fostered an argument, still
heatedly pursued by some legal scholars today, over what the Fourth
Amendment really protects against. There are those who claim that the
Fourth Amendment is divided into two independent clauses: the first
prohibits unreasonable searches and seizures, and the second defines the
requirements for a search warrant, should one be requested. Those press-
ing this interpretation argue that for a search to be reasonable, it need
not be based on a warrant.[27]

The Supreme Court has not adopted this view, although a number
of justices, both past and present, led by former justice Byron White,
strongly supported it. Their approach, usually in dissent, was to say, "The
question is not whether a warrant is necessary, but whether the search,
itself, was reasonable."[28] However, Justice Stewart, writing for the majority, rejected this view as sloppy and of little guidance to law enforcement
officers. He wrote that "a warrantless search and seizure is per se unreasonable, unless it fits within certain well-defined exceptions."[29]

Does this disagreement matter? Profoundly. To hold that the
framers of the Constitution were willing to define a warrantless search
and seizure—not compelled by exigent circumstances—as reasonable
runs in the face of the history we have reviewed and defies the logic and

fervor of the revolutionary leaders. From the debates over the issue of a Bill of Rights, it is clear that what the House Committee wanted to do in the Fourth Amendment was to prohibit general warrants, which became so hated in England and the colonies in the eighteenth century. With that as the goal of the amendment, certainly a search without any warrant at all, and not required by exigency, would not have been acceptable.[30] Even in the Wilkes case, the secretary of state had issued a general warrant, which was condemned by Lord Camden as illegal. It would be absurd to argue that Lord Camden would have held that a search and seizure without any warrant would be good. Lord Camden ruled that for a search to be valid, a warrant must be issued by a judicial officer having jurisdiction, and it must be a special warrant on probable cause, particularly describing the individual or place to be searched and things to be seized.

This was exactly the reason for Madison's first wording of the Fourth Amendment, which was approved by the House Committee. It assumed that there would be a warrant to authorize searches, but it prohibited general warrants by requiring the warrant to be based on probable cause and particularly describing the person and place to be searched. Though the Supreme Court adopted Stewart's view of the Fourth Amendment, it permitted certain well-defined exceptions to the warrant requirement, based on exigent circumstances that made seeking a warrant futile. A number of these exceptions, such as a search incident to a lawful arrest, were also recognized in English common law. However, in more recent times, the Supreme Court has allowed additional exceptions to such an extent that they have mostly swallowed up the prohibition of warrantless searches.

CHAPTER 4

The Plate-Glass Duty Fraud Case

In order to ascertain the nature of the proceedings intended by the Fourth Amendment to the Constitution under the term unreasonable searches and seizures, it is only necessary to recall the contemporary or the recent history of the controversies on the subject, both in this country and in England.

Justice Bradley in Boyd v. United States, *116 U.S. 616*
(1885)

Despite the flame of fire James Otis must have been in his argument against writs of assistance, and which John Adams said sparked the Revolution and freedom, the Bill of Rights' Fourth Amendment protection against unreasonable searches and seizures did not become an issue before the U.S. Supreme Court until close to one hundred years after the ratification of that crucial amendment. Why was this so?[1] Were there no searches and seizures by federal officers during the first hundred years of governance under the new Constitution by the new federal government? Apparently, there were none as occurred in England before the Revolution or as we know them today. The only federal police in the first half of the nineteenth century were U.S. marshals, authorized by Congress in the Federal Judiciary Act of 1789. Very few federal crimes were enacted by a Congress that was extremely sensitive to its limited powers and to the hostility of the states to the federal government's intrusion into the criminal law enforcement of the states. Congress did not have power to adopt the English common law crimes into federal law. It needed a specific federal purpose to define a federal crime, such as treason against the United States or a murder committed on federal government property. Congress was not loath to enact federal criminal law where it had jurisdiction. The Alien and Sedition Acts, enacted during John Adams's administration, were its most notorious criminal legislation. This legislation was used to suppress public criticism against the Federalists in office by the Republican Party headed by Thomas Jefferson. Clearly in violation of the First Amendment of the new Constitution, these prosecutions tainted Adams's presidency.

Representing a sovereign country, however, Congress, early in its history, did enact customs, trade, and duty laws and authorized searches of vessels at sea and other places at the border to enforce these laws. These searches could be made without probable cause or warrants, consistent with the law of sovereignty recognized in England and other nations. Later, Supreme Court decisions reconciled these warrantless searches with the Fourth Amendment requirements by saying that they were consistent with sovereign rights at the border and that they had been passed by the same Congress that had approved the Fourth Amendment.

Of course, the states could and did adopt the English common law of crimes, and their legislatures added more crimes to their penal codes. However, there were no organized state or local police forces in existence, either before or after the Revolution. The colonies, and later the states, had adopted the English system of sheriffs and constables, who could do little more than try to keep the peace and make arrests. Indeed, actual law enforcement was a private matter. All adult male citizens of a community were required to share, in turn, the responsibility of watching for crime. Richer citizens could hire others to take the watch for them. Merchants often hired private watchmen to tour the streets at night. History has remembered the watchmen as those who called out, "Nine o'clock, clear, and all is well!" As in early England, private citizens took on the responsibility for seeing that criminals were caught by chasing them and arresting them. The prosecution was by the private victim of the crime, the system of public prosecutors not having been established yet.

The state courts did, in the late eighteenth century and early nineteenth century, have occasion to review searches and seizures by constables and sheriffs. The rulings emphasized the need for particularity in describing the place to be searched and the thing to be seized. For example, a warrant authorizing search for stolen property "in all places where the complainant suspects it may be found" was held to be too extensive and illegal.[2] A warrant describing the goods to be searched for as "goods, wares, and merchandise" was held to be insufficient as a particular description of the things to be seized.[3]

These early state cases provide no evidence of state governments or legislatures seeking to authorize general or warrantless searches. Indeed, a Massachusetts court ruling in 1838 held that the meaning of the words "unreasonable searches and seizures" was determined by the warrant clause that followed. Thus, to be reasonable, the court held, a search had to be based on probable cause and a proper warrant.[4] Early on, a number of state courts held that the Fourth Amendment to the U.S. Constitution did not apply to the states. The U.S. Supreme Court did not challenge these decisions, and, as we shall see, later agreed with them. Therefore, there were no Fourth Amendment search and seizure questions for the Supreme Court to review.

Not until 1886. The case the Supreme Court chose to be its first Fourth Amendment case was not a criminal case. It was a civil fraud action for the forfeiture to the government of fifty-two cases of plate glass that had been seized by Treasury agents at the Port of New York City. In 1882, the federal government had begun construction of a new post office and courthouse at Ninth and Chestnut Streets in Philadelphia. The supervising federal architect had designed the windows for French plate glass. He requested bids from glass companies and awarded the contract to the lowest bidder, E. A. Boyd & Sons, importers and dealers in plate glass in New York City.[5] Edward A. Boyd, the father and head of the business, had emigrated from Ireland while still a young man. He was able to get a job with a glass import firm and later became a partner of the firm, which then traded under the name of Platt & Boyd. Subsequently, Edward Boyd took over the firm and brought his son, George, into the business as a partner, trading as E. A. Boyd & Sons.

The construction of the post office fell behind schedule, and the supervising architect was fearful that he would violate the appropriation statute's peremptory requirement that the courthouse be ready by July 1, 1883, and the post office by October 1883. The architect increased the pace of construction and found that he needed the French plate glass for the windows sooner than Boyd could order them from abroad.[6] Ordinarily, Boyd would order the correctly measured French plate glass from a supplier in St. Helen's, near Liverpool, in England, and the glass would be sent by ship across the Atlantic to the Port of New York. This glass was subject to a hefty duty on arrival at the port. Boyd's contract with the federal government, however, permitted him to import the glass for the post office and courthouse free of federal duty.

Boyd offered to ship to Philadelphia a sufficient quantity of French plate glass, which he then had in his inventory for other contracts, and on which he had paid the federal duty. In return, he requested authority from the federal government to replace this inventory glass with an equivalent amount of glass to be imported duty-free.[7] This was readily agreed to.

What started out as a seemingly cooperative effort by Boyd, and an agreement that he could replace the glass duty-free, ended, instead, in the seizure by Treasury agents of the new shipment of glass from St. Helen's to Boyd while it still was at the port. Moreover, the United States attorney for New York filed a civil fraud action for forfeiture of the seized glass to the United States.

What had happened? As in most cases, there were two sides to the story. The United States attorney was Elihu Root, recently appointed by President Chester Alan Arthur, who had instructed Root to "make a success of that position." Not only did Root make a success of it, but he went on to become one of the most accomplished lawyers and statesmen in U.S. history. He became secretary of war and secretary of state under President Theodore Roosevelt and later was elected a U.S. senator. In 1912, Root received the Nobel Peace Prize for his brilliant and successful diplomatic negotiations with Japan.

Root charged that Boyd had exploited the government agreement to allow Boyd to replace the inventory glass with an equivalent amount of imported glass duty-free. He accused Boyd of fraudulently using the duty-free permit the Treasury Department had given him to import not just an equivalent amount of the glass Boyd shipped to Philadelphia for the post office building but, instead, a much larger supply of glass. Through this scheme, Root claimed, Boyd had defrauded the U.S. government of the large amount of duty owed on the glass imported in excess of that needed to replace the amount he had sent to Philadelphia.[8]

Boyd vehemently denied that he had been fraudulent. He insisted that it was wrong to determine the equivalence of his replacement imported glass to the amount of glass he sent to Philadelphia by measuring only the exact amount of glass he sent. Rather, he claimed, the determination had to include the amount of inventory glass he had to waste by cutting this glass down to provide the smaller-sized glass needed for the post office building.[9] Further, he argued, the government had to credit him for the large amount of glass breakage in the glass shipped from St. Helen's.

To obtain evidence of the disparity that Root claimed existed between the amount of glass provided by Boyd for the post office building and the amount Boyd imported as replacement under the duty-free permit, Root obtained a court order compelling Boyd to produce his invoice for the glass he had imported. Boyd's lawyer, Richard S.

Newcombe, challenged the legality of the court subpoena on the ground that it violated Boyd's privilege against self-incrimination. Newcombe was a successful New York lawyer and politician. He had once been the partner of Judge Albert Cardozo, one of the "Tammany judges" who was forced out of office by the good government lawyers of the newly formed Association of the Bar of the City of New York. Judge Cardozo was also the father of Benjamin Cardozo, who later distinguished himself as one of the great justices of the U.S. Supreme Court. Newcombe was not destined to reach the heights Root did. His controversial political reputation went ahead of him, and New York Governor Grover Cleveland passed him over for appointment as district attorney to fill the vacancy in that office caused by the death of the incumbent. Nevertheless, Newcombe's success in his law practice made him a very wealthy man. He died during surgery at the age of forty-seven in 1891.

The district court judge overruled Newcombe's self-incrimination objection and ordered Boyd to produce the invoice. At first, Boyd claimed he could not find the invoice, but under prodding by the court, he cabled his English supplier for a duplicate invoice, which he received and gave to the court, over objection.

Boyd's reason for his compliance with the court's order to produce the invoice was to avoid the consequences of not complying. The court's order was specifically authorized by the Internal Revenue Act of 1874, which provided, further, that if a party in a civil revenue proceeding refused to produce books and papers ordered to be produced by the court, the refusal would be deemed to constitute a confession of the government's allegations in the suit. In Boyd's case, his refusal would have defeated his claim, and on the basis of it, the court would have condemned the glass shipment and ordered it forfeited to the U.S. government. By advising Boyd to comply with the order under protest, Newcombe believed he would have the opportunity to challenge the government's case on the merits, and if he lost, he had preserved his right to appeal on the ground that the 1874 law unconstitutionally compelled Boyd to produce incriminating evidence against himself.

The trial judge took the position that the Internal Revenue Act of 1874 was specifically written to avoid the self-incrimination problem. Ordinarily, if a party refused to comply with a court subpoena, the court could hold the individual in contempt and jail him until he did comply. This coercive power has been considered to invoke the Fifth Amendment prohibition that no person may be compelled to be a witness against himself. On the other hand, the judge said, the statute took the contempt power away from the judge for noncompliance of his order, and substituted, instead, the presumption of confession, certainly not as coercive as a jail term.

On the basis of the evidence Boyd produced, the jury found for the government, and the trial court ordered the glass forfeited to the United States. The Court of Appeals for the Second Circuit affirmed the judgment of forfeiture, and Boyd appealed, through a writ of error, to the U.S. Supreme Court.

United States Attorney Root was not satisfied with winning the civil forfeiture case alone. He obtained a grand jury indictment against Edward Boyd and his son, George, for criminal fraud. In doing so, Root placed himself in a contradictory position. In the civil tax case, Root had argued that Boyd had not been compelled to incriminate himself by complying with the court order to produce the invoice because it was a civil case and Boyd had suffered no penalty. He claimed that the forfeiture was not a penalty against Boyd, but only against the quantity of imported glass.[10] Root pointed out that the case was captioned "United States v. 52 Cases of Glass," which is known to the law as an action *in rem*, or an action against the thing. Indeed, he said, Boyd had voluntarily injected himself into the suit as a claimant for the glass.

Now, in the criminal case against the Boyds, Root could not make that argument. He was seeking a criminal conviction and punishment based on the evidence Boyd had been compelled to produce.

Despite this inconsistency, father and son were convicted without this issue's being raised.

At the sentencing proceedings, there was an emotional moment. Defense counsel Newcombe told the court he wished to make a brief statement on behalf of the father, Edward A. Boyd, at his desire. "Young Boyd," he said, "was merely a nominal partner of the firm. He had been employed as a boy in the store, and afterwards as a clerk, and had grown up in the business with his father. The son had only acted at his direction." The judge, in response to this plea, said he would not send the son to prison, but would impose upon him the moderate fine of one thousand dollars.

Then, turning to the father, the judge said, "You are not a young man. There is no doubt that you are guilty of the frauds charged. There is reason to suppose also that you are guilty of other frauds. It is the case of an intelligent man who has deliberately entered upon a course of fraud for the sake of gain. I shall impose no fine on you. As a meet punishment for you, and that it may be a warning to others, I shall inflict a sentence of imprisonment. You were not induced by want, or by temptation of others, but by a desire of gain. Your sentence is two years imprisonment, and it is ordered to be executed in the King's County Penitentiary."

The shock of prison life so traumatized Boyd that his physical and mental health began to erode. His legal fortune began to change for the better, however, after the U.S. Supreme Court held arguments in his civil forfeiture case. The Court reversed the judgment of forfeiture on the ground that the Internal Revenue Act of 1874 unconstitutionally violated his protections under both the Fourth and Fifth Amendments. Justice Joseph Bradley, a poor New York farm boy who had worked his own way up to become a leading member at the bar and to be appointed by President U. S. Grant to the Supreme Court, wrote the opinion for the Court.

Justice Bradley's opinion in *Boyd v. U.S.*[11] held that the Act of 1874, and the court's order under it, violated Boyd's Fourth Amendment protection against unreasonable search and seizure. It was the Court's first interpretation of the Fourth Amendment. But under the facts, how could there have been a Fourth Amendment violation? There had not been any physical entry into or search of Boyd's home or office or any seizure of any of his effects. It was a court order, in the nature of a subpoena, issued under the Act of 1874, that compelled Boyd to personally produce his invoice in court. Never before, either in state cases or in English cases, had such an order been equated to a search and seizure.

Bradley, however, went beyond the history and language of the Fourth Amendment and held that the subpoena amounted to the same thing because the result was the same as if Treasury agents had entered Boyd's office and seized the invoice. Bradley reasoned that Boyd's production of the invoice was really a seizure of it because Boyd had no other choice, having been coerced to produce the evidence under penalty of forfeiture if he did not. But even this reasoning did not support a Fourth Amendment violation. Instead, it provided a basis for the Court to find, as it also did, that Boyd had been compelled to produce incriminating evidence against himself, in violation of his Fifth Amendment rights.

Perhaps what best explains Bradley's unorthodox view was his heavy reliance on the only precedent he could find, Lord Camden's opinion in *Entick v. Carrington* in 1765. However, *Entick*, unlike *Boyd*, did involve a physical entry into and search of a printer's home and a seizure of all his private books and papers by the messengers of the secretary of state. Lord Camden condemned this search and seizure on the ground that it had been conducted under an unlawful general warrant. Justice Bradley must have relied on Lord Camden's emphatic statement, in referring to the seized papers, that "papers are often the dearest property a man can have," and, if the law permitted their seizure, "it would destroy all comforts of society."

There also was language in Lord Camden's opinion that alluded to the English law's prohibition against self-incrimination. Lord Camden said, "The law never forces evidence from the party in whose power it is." This statement was not directed to the search and seizure question, however, but to the validity of the government's strategy in authorizing a search of a citizen's house for evidence of a libel before it had been published. If such a search were proper, Lord Camden observed, "Half the kingdom would be guilty."

Despite this language in *Entick*, which Justice Bradley may have found supportive of his Fourth Amendment interpretation, it is clear that Lord Camden's ruling was directed to an unlawful search and seizure of the traditional kind. He held the general warrant to be abhorrent because it permitted the government's agents to enter people's homes and property at their sole discretion, without any judicial supervision or specification. Lord Camden spoke eloquently on this subject. He said, "Our law holds the property of every man so sacred, that no man can set his foot upon his neighbor's close without his leave." It was this sacred property and privacy right that was symbolized by the legend "every man's home is his castle" and that William Pitt enshrined in his statement in Parliament that no matter how humble a person's home may be, the king of England and all his force may not enter it without his permission.

Lord Camden's emphasis on the sacredness of private papers in a person's home may have formed the benchmark for the theory, later adopted by the U.S. Supreme Court, and still later rejected, that even a validly issued search warrant could not authorize a search for and seizure of private books and papers, or mere evidence of crime. Under this view, a search warrant could only permit the seizure of items the government has a paramount right to have, such as stolen goods, contraband, and unlawful weapons.

Justice Bradley accommodated the distinction between the Fourth Amendment and the Fifth Amendment by holding that, in *Boyd*, the Fourth and Fifth Amendments ran into each other. However, Bradley's stretched interpretation of the Fourth Amendment could only lead to confusion over search and seizure law. His opinion would have been more consistent with history and a clearer guide to government agents if he had reversed the forfeiture judgment on the ground of the Fifth

Amendment alone. His opinion amply supported such a ruling. Bradley rejected the government's and the trial court's arguments that Boyd was not compelled to produce the incriminating evidence because the court's order provided no sanction for noncompliance, such as contempt of court. Bradley found it sanction enough for Boyd to be faced with forfeiture of a substantial amount of expensive glass if he refused to produce the evidence.

In later cases, the Supreme Court distanced itself from Bradley's use of the Fourth Amendment in court subpoena cases. These opinions distinguished between a subpoena compelling the production of private books and papers, which raised a Fifth Amendment issue,[12] and a search of a person's home or office to seize private books and papers, which raised a Fourth Amendment issue.

Boyd's victory in the civil forfeiture case in the Supreme Court had no legal impact on his conviction and sentence of imprisonment in the criminal case. This was so despite the fact that the criminal conviction was based on the same evidence that Bradley had found was unlawfully obtained. Other than the availability of a civil action against the government agents for damages resulting from an unlawful search and seizure, neither the Court nor Congress had devised a stronger remedy for such government illegality.

By the time of the Supreme Court decision, Boyd's health had deteriorated so much that the physician of the penitentiary feared Boyd would not survive further imprisonment. Dr. Joseph D. Bryant, the prison doctor, wrote a report on Boyd's poor health condition to President Cleveland, who issued a pardon to Boyd on humanitarian grounds, just two months after Boyd won his case in the Supreme Court.

The president did not mention the Supreme Court ruling, or base his decision on anything other than Boyd's health. Boyd, however, was never to enjoy his freedom. Just two months after his pardon, he died of the respiratory failure the prison doctor had diagnosed. He had spent ten months in prison out of his sentence of two years.

CHAPTER 5

The Exclusionary Rule

The effect of the 4th Amendment is to put the courts of the United States and Federal officials, in the exercise of their power and authority, under limitations and restraints as to the exercise of such power and authority, and to forever secure the people against all unreasonable searches and seizures under guise of law . . . and the duty of giving [this protection] force and effect is obligatory upon all entrusted under our Federal system with the enforcement of the law.

Justice William R. Day in Weeks v. United States, *32 U.S. 383*
(1914)

Lord Camden's ruling in the Wilkes set of cases and Justice Bradley's ruling in Boyd were hailed, and still are hailed today, as great victories for the freedom of the individual. What kind of victories were they? Both Wilkes and Boyd were convicted of crimes and sentenced to prison on the basis of the same evidence Camden and Bradley condemned as unlawful and obtained by the government in violation of one of the most sacred rights of the individual. The only remedy they received for the government's illegality was money damages in Wilkes's case and the return of property in Boyd's case.

Why did not Lord Camden or Justice Bradley consider the remedy of excluding the illegally obtained evidence in the criminal case, and thus prevent a conviction? Wouldn't such a ruling teach the government agents the lesson that they will not be permitted to benefit from their own illegal conduct? Why did neither Wilkes nor Boyd even raise this issue? In the eighteenth, nineteenth, and first half of the twentieth centuries, there were some clear answers to this incongruity in search and seizure law. These answers were the result of the courts' balancing of two important values: the need to punish criminals through convictions on probative and reliable evidence and the need to protect people from unreasonable government searches and seizures.

The courts split the baby and chose money damages in a civil torts suit for the purpose of protecting against unreasonable searches and seizures. They chose to admit the same illegally obtained evidence against the wronged citizen in the criminal case because of the strong public policy in enforcing the criminal law. Besides, they defended their public policy position by pointing out that evidence obtained by the government through an illegal search and seizure was just as competent and probative as if it had been obtained legally.[1]

There was logic to this reasoning. The reliability of the evidence of seditious libel and of obscenity against Wilkes had not been altered by the unlawful search and seizure by the secretary of state's messengers under the general warrant. Likewise, the content of the incriminating invoice for the imported glass remained unchanged by the fact that Boyd was unlawfully compelled by the court order to turn it over.

Surely, the courts agreed, the government agents must pay for their illegal conduct. But why should "the criminal go free just because the constable blundered?" This was the question posed by Benjamin Cardozo (later a justice of the U.S. Supreme Court) when, as chief justice of the New York Court of Appeals in the 1920s, he refused to exclude illegally obtained evidence in a criminal case.[2] "Both the government agent and the criminal should be punished," Cardozo said.

Was Cardozo right that the constable would also be punished? During this early period in English and American history, the targets of this unlawful conduct by the government often were prominent and respectable citizens with good standing in the community. Certainly this was true of both Wilkes and Boyd. Hefty damages that might affect future government conduct were more likely in these civil suits from jurors who could readily identify with and be sympathetic to the complainants. As we shall see, in the second half of the twentieth century, the targets of illegal searches and seizures mostly were the poor, who were charged with crimes the public hated or feared. In sharp contrast to the Wilkes and Boyd cases, the jurors in these later cases refused to identify with these unworthy defendants. What comes of the policy of deterring future government misconduct when the government does not have to pay damages?

Another rationale used by courts in refusing to suppress illegally seized evidence had to do with the efficiency of trying criminal cases and moving the docket. Both state and federal courts held that the criminal trial would not be stopped to consider the collateral question of how otherwise reliable and probative evidence was acquired by the government.

This was the state of the law in 1911, when Fremont Weeks had the misfortune to be arrested for illegally selling lottery tickets. It was a trivial criminal matter that resulted from the worst case of bad luck petty gambler Weeks had ever suffered. It all started in Jones Department Store in Kansas City when a store detective noticed Mrs. Weeks slipping several pairs of kid gloves inside some bundles she was carrying.[3]

Mrs. Weeks was arrested and taken to the police station. From there, she sent a warning note to her husband, evidently fearing a followup police search of their home. The police intercepted and read the note.[4] City detectives and a U.S. marshal went to the Weekses' home without a warrant and thoroughly searched it. They found what appeared to them to be additional shoplifted items. Worse for Fremont Weeks, they seized a large number of illegal lottery tickets and some letters and papers having to do with Weeks's selling the lottery tickets. The officers also seized about a hundred other private papers that had nothing to do with the sale of lottery tickets, such as personal correspondence, insurance policies, stock certificates, personal notebooks, and real estate deeds. Weeks was indicted for the federal offense of illegally sending lottery tickets through the U.S. mail.

The case was assigned to U.S. District Judge Arba S. Van Valkenburgh. Judge Van Valkenburgh was born near Syracuse, New York, in 1862. Like Justice Bradley, he had been born on a farm. Although, he, too, made it to the top of his profession, he had more help than Bradley. His father was one of the principal founders of the Republican Party.

Before trial, Weeks's defense lawyer, Martin J. O'Donnell, moved in the U.S. District Court for the return of Weeks's property unlawfully taken from his home. Although Judge Van Valkenburgh agreed that the warrantless search had been unlawful, he denied the motion because it referred to items he found pertinent to guilt and needed by the United States attorney's case for conviction. However, he generously granted the motion as to those seized items that were not incriminating or needed by the prosecutor for trial. Judge Van Valkenburgh was supported in this ruling by precedent in the U.S. Supreme Court and in state courts, which had held that even if evidence is obtained by an unlawful search and seizure, it still is admissible against the accused if it is otherwise competent and relevant.

Weeks was required to stand trial. The jury convicted him on the basis of the illegally seized evidence, and Judge Van Valkenburgh sentenced him to six months' imprisonment in the Johnson County Jail in Warrensburg, Missouri, and imposed a fine of one hundred dollars. Weeks appealed his conviction to the U.S. Supreme Court on a writ of error claiming his conviction and sentence violated his Fourth Amendment rights.

Weeks's lawyer, Martin J. O'Donnell, had an uphill fight. The precedents were against his position that the illegally seized evidence had to be returned to Weeks and not used against him at his trial. As we have seen, even in Boyd, on which O'Donnell relied heavily, the incriminating evidence, which the U.S. Supreme Court had held to have been illegally obtained, was permitted to be used in his criminal trial, resulting in his conviction.

O'Donnell, in a forcefully argued sixty-seven-page brief, attacked head-on the indifference courts had shown to the use of illegally seized evidence. He argued that exclusion of the unlawfully obtained evidence was essential for the enforcement of the Fourth Amendment. "How, therefore," he asked, "can the rights of defendants 'to be secure in their persons, houses, papers, and effects' be asserted by and granted to them as the Constitution guarantees, in this Court? Can it be done by placing in the hands of the government officials charged by law with the prosecution of defendants as offenders against its laws, the fruits of this unlawful invasion of Constitutional rights of defendants by the agents of the Government?"

Assistant Attorney General Winifred T. Dennison replied for the government. He used less than a printed page and curtly informed the Supreme Court that the issues Weeks raised were no longer open for review but had been decided against Weeks by precedents of the Court.

The members of the Supreme Court who heard arguments in the Weeks case on December 2, 1913, were especially illustrious. They included justices with some of the best legal minds in the history of the Court. Prominent among them were Associate Justices Oliver Wendell Holmes Jr. and Charles Evans Hughes. Associate Justice William R. Day was assigned to write the opinion of the Court.

Justice Day was born on April 17, 1849, in Ravenna, Ohio. His family was distinguished by producing, over four generations, members who held high judicial office. His maternal great-grandfather had been chief justice of the Supreme Court of Connecticut. His grandfather was a justice on the Ohio Supreme Court. His father was chief justice of the Ohio Supreme Court. There was only one career for young William Day, and he took it by storm.

In his opinion for the Court, Justice Day reversed Weeks's conviction and sentence. He held that Judge Van Valkenburgh had erroneously denied Weeks's petition for the return of his illegally seized papers and had also erroneously permitted these papers to be used in evidence against Weeks. Justice Day's opinion for the Court was unprecedented. The opinion did not overrule its precedent in *Adams v. New York*, 192 U.S. 585 (1904), where the Court had ruled that a trial judge does not have to consider in the midst of trial the collateral question of whether illegally seized evidence should be excluded but should admit the evidence if it is otherwise competent and relevant. Instead, Justice Day distinguished *Adams* and other similar cases in state and lower federal courts by finding that Weeks petitioned for the return of the seized papers before trial and this prevented the application of the rule followed in those cases.

Though this distinction permitted Justice Day to maintain the appearance of symmetry of the Supreme Court decisions in Fourth Amendment cases, it was flatly a diversion to permit the Court to announce a new rule of exclusion from the trial of evidence obtained by an unlawful search and seizure. This is so because Justice Day wrote that not only should the tainted papers have been returned to Weeks, they should not have been used at all as evidence against him at his trial. What was distinctively a departure from the prior cases was the Court's decision to make the exclusion of illegally seized evidence a necessary remedy for violations by government agents of the Fourth Amendment.

Apparently, the Court no longer believed that the remedy of a civil suit for money damages against the erring government agent was sufficient for the effective enforcement of Fourth Amendment guarantees. Also, the Court held that it was the Fourth Amendment that demanded the exclusion of illegally obtained evidence. It did not rely on the Fifth Amendment's prohibition of self-incrimination as the Court did in *Boyd*.[5]

For the first time, the Court included itself and the other federal courts in the obligation to enforce the Bill of Rights in their own proceedings. The courts could not separate themselves from unconstitutional acts by federal law enforcement officials on the ground that the wrongdoing was committed by those officials and not by the courts. According to Justice Day, a judge's admission of illegally seized evidence in the trial proceedings was, itself, an additional violation of the Fourth Amendment.

The clear rationale for this change in direction by the Court is the Court's recognition, as expressed in Justice Day's opinion, that the Fourth Amendment amounts to nothing more than meaningless words on paper without a remedy for its violation that has teeth in it. This is the unambiguous meaning of Justice Day's words:

> If letters and private documents can thus be seized and held and used in evidence against a citizen accused of an offense, the protection of the Fourth Amendment declaring his right to be secure against such searches and seizures is of no value, and, so far as those thus placed are concerned, might as well be stricken from the Constitution. The efforts of the courts and their officials to bring the guilty to punishment, praiseworthy as they are, are not to be aided by the sacrifice of those great principles established by years of endeavor and suffering which have resulted in their embodiment in the fundamental law of the land.

After such dramatic and forceful language, Justice Day's opinion closes with a whimper. Weeks is not home free. In addition to the U.S. marshal, local Kansas City detectives also participated in the warrantless seizure of the incriminating papers against Weeks. Justice Day's ruling prohibited these papers from being used in evidence against Weeks in a federal courtroom. He made it clear, however, that the Court's ruling would have no effect in a state prosecution based on the same illegally seized evidence. Justice Day wrote, "What remedies the defendant may have against them [the local and state officials] we need not inquire, as the Fourth Amendment is not directed to individual misconduct of such officials. Its limitations reach the federal government and its agencies."

Insofar as federal law enforcement officials were concerned, the Court, in *Weeks*, laid down the gauntlet. It created a high-profile controversy for years to come. Indeed, the debate over the exclusionary rule is as hot today as it was in 1914. This is where we now go, to the aftermath of *Weeks* and the story of that turbulent debate. It took nearly half a century for *Weeks*'s exclusionary rule to become part of every person's armor against unlawful government intrusion, in both state and federal proceedings. Unfortunately, this triumph, which was resented by law enforcement agencies and conservative judges, sowed the seeds of its downfall. As we shall see, *Weeks*'s exclusionary rule, meant to give effective meaning to the guarantee of the Fourth Amendment, barely survives today.

But first we must take a side trip to prepare us for the longer journey. How could it be, as Justice Day said in *Weeks*, that the Fourth Amendment, and for that matter all of the Bill of Rights in the U.S. Constitution, did not protect all Americans, particularly those who are victims of constitutional abuse by state and local police officials? On its face this is a ridiculous position, until one reconstructs the serious tensions that existed between the states and the federal government at the time the Bill of Rights was adopted.

Why did the states protest so much against the absence of a bill of rights in the U.S. Constitution during the ratification debates, if the guaranteed rights they demanded would not apply to state proceedings? Simply because the states feared the potential tyranny of a strong central federal government and wanted to limit the power of that government. As state leaders saw it, the new chief executive of the United States, though called a president, could become a George III. They did not believe their citizens needed to be protected by the federal Constitution against state official action for the reasons that each state had its own constitutional protections, and state citizens, through a much more local political process, controlled the behavior of their state leaders, including law enforcement officials.

After the Civil War and the adoption of the Fourteenth Amendment, the vaunted law enforcement autonomy of the states became threatened. To help implement the Thirteenth Amendment, which abolished slavery, Section 1 of the Fourteenth Amendment declared:

> All persons born or naturalized in the United States, and subject to the jurisdiction thereof, are citizens of the United States and of the State wherein they reside. No State shall make or enforce any law which shall abridge the privileges or immunities of citizens of the United States; nor shall any State deprive any person of life, liberty or property, without due process of law; nor deny to any person within its jurisdiction the equal protection of the laws.

Thus, the Fourteenth Amendment now added to the U.S. Constitution protections for citizens against certain conduct of their own state officials. But what state conduct was prohibited under the Fourteenth Amendment? The important issue for us is whether it prohibited the conduct protected against by the Bill of Rights of the U.S. Constitution. More particularly, for our purposes, did it prohibit violations of the Fourth Amendment by state officials?

Based on Supreme Court precedent, the federal Constitution's Fourth Amendment had not been considered a privilege or immunity of citizens of the United States in relation to state officials' actions and proceedings. Nor was the fact that state citizens did not have the same protections against their state officials that they had against federal officials considered a denial of the equal protection of the laws. Though these clauses of the Fourteenth Amendment were cited as supporting the application of Fourth Amendment protections in state criminal cases, the clause that received the most judicial attention was the prohibition against depriving any person of life, liberty, or property without due process of law. This is the ancient protection dating to King John's commitment to the barons in the Magna Carta in 1215.

The Supreme Court could have interpreted the due process clause of the Fourteenth Amendment to include the protections of the U.S. Bill of Rights,[6] particularly the Fourth Amendment's fundamental guarantee against the kind of abusive official action that helped to spark the Revolution in the first place. But this was not to be.

Throughout the nineteenth century there were references in state and federal court opinions to the U.S. Bill of Rights not being applicable to state court proceedings. However, it was not until the Supreme Court, in the first part of the twentieth century, began to review whether individual provisions of the Bill of Rights were included in the due process clause of the Fourteenth Amendment that the Court solidified its position against inclusion.

This important issue arose in Connecticut in 1936, when the Supreme Court of Connecticut held that the prohibition against double jeopardy in the Fifth Amendment did not control Connecticut state cases. The Connecticut court's decision was upheld by the U.S. Supreme Court in *Palko v. Connecticut*.[7] The Supreme Court had earlier held, in *Twining v. New Jersey*,[8] that the Fifth Amendment prohibition against a person being compelled to be a witness against himself did not prevent a state court from commenting on the failure of a criminal defendant to take the stand in his own defense. In both cases, the Supreme Court specifically ruled that the due process clause of the Fourteenth Amendment did not automatically import to the states all the provisions of the U.S. Bill of Rights. The Court said that in each case it must inquire whether the official conduct prohibited by a specific Bill of Rights protection is sufficiently grave to amount to a violation of due process. The standard of gravity the Court employed in *Palko* was extremely high. To be prohibited under the due process clause, the Court held, the conduct must violate "fundamental principles of fairness," must be "incompatible with a system of ordered liberty," and must be one which "people in a civilized society would not tolerate." The Court ruled that double jeopardy protection did not meet this standard.

Similarly, using the same abstract and lofty standards, the Supreme Court in 1947, in *Adamson v. California*,[9] reaffirmed its ruling in *Twining v. New Jersey* that a violation by state officials of the Fifth Amendment protection against self-incrimination did not offend the due process clause of the Fourteenth Amendment. These rulings created anomalous situations where evidence illegally obtained by federal police could be handed over to state prosecutors who were free to use that evidence in a state criminal case. It was known as the "silver platter" doctrine.

Justice Felix Frankfurter justified these rulings of the Court on the ground they were derived by careful analysis, reasoning, and objective study by the Court in each case of the proper application of the due process clause. His careful analysis and objectivity vanished, however, when California police pumped the stomach of a narcotics suspect they saw swallow some capsules as they approached to arrest him. The defendant was convicted on the basis of the narcotics found in the substance pumped out of his stomach. Reversing the conviction on the ground that the police conduct violated the due process clause, in *Rochin v. California*,[10] Frankfurter emotionally declared in the opinion, "The conduct shocked the conscience!" However, Frankfurter's ruling offered no indication that the Supreme Court was softening on the question of applying the Bill of Rights to state official conduct. This was the state of the law in 1949 when Justice Frankfurter wrote the majority opinion for the Court in *Wolf v. Colorado*.[11]

On April 25, 1944, the Denver, Colorado, district attorney's office received an anonymous tip that there was a woman suffering from the aftereffects of an abortion in room 602 of the Cosmopolitan Hotel. Investigators and prosecutors from the district attorney's office went to the room and found Miss Gertrude Martin, who told them she had aborted her unwanted pregnancy. She said that she had gone to Dr. Julius A. Wolf before and after the abortion.[12] These officials then went to Dr. Wolf's office and entered it without an arrest warrant or search warrant. They arrested Dr. Wolf and seized two appointment books from his desk. The books contained the names, addresses, and telephone numbers of his patients.

All of the patients were women. The police contacted each of them and questioned them, discovering that each had received an illegal abortion. Some became state witnesses against Dr. Wolf and Dr. Andrew Montgomery, who had actually performed the abortions. Dr. Wolf was charged as a co-conspirator and participant in the examination of the women before and after their abortions.

Wolf's counsel moved to have the appointment books suppressed on the ground that they had been obtained by an illegal search and seizure in violation of Wolf's right to due process. The trial court ruled against the motion and held that the evidence in the books was admissible against Wolf. Both Wolf and Montgomery were convicted by the jury, and the judge imposed sentences of imprisonment. The Colorado Supreme Court upheld the convictions, but the U.S. Supreme Court agreed to review the case, and argument before the Court was heard on October 19, 1948.

The *Wolf* case marked the first time the U.S. Supreme Court directly addressed the question of whether the federal exclusionary rule adopted in the *Weeks* case applied to state criminal cases as well. Philip Hornbein, a prominent Denver trial lawyer who later turned down an appointment to the Colorado Supreme Court, argued that *Weeks* must be applied by the Court to the states as a due process requirement because the Fourth Amendment expressed fundamental liberty rights of the people. He even told the Court that "freedom from search and seizure without warrant is a basic right of Englishmen dating back to Magna Carta." The attorney general of Colorado labeled the *Weeks* rule of exclusion only a federal rule of evidence that was inapplicable to Colorado, which followed the contrary common law rule as determined by the Supreme Court of Colorado.

On a vote of six to three, the Supreme Court upheld the conviction.[13] Writing for the majority, Justice Felix Frankfurter dissected the issue into two parts. First, he addressed the issue of whether the Fourth Amendment itself applied to the states under the due process clause of the Fourteenth Amendment. Police unlawful conduct would fall under the due process clause, Frankfurter said, if the rights violated were basic to a free society. He found that the protection of the Fourth Amendment was so basic. "The knock on the door," he wrote, "whether by day or by night, as a prelude to a search, without the authority of law but solely on the authority of the police, did not need the commentary of recent history [Nazi Germany] to be condemned as inconsistent with the conception of human rights enshrined in the history and the basic constitutional documents of English-speaking peoples."

However, the second part of the issue in *Wolf*, whether the remedy for a violation of the Fourth Amendment required, under due process, the exclusion of the unlawfully seized evidence, Frankfurter thought called for an entirely different answer. To determine whether a rule of exclusion was implicit in the concept of ordered liberty and fundamental fairness, Frankfurter looked to the law of England and the majority of the states in the United States. He found that these jurisdictions had rejected the exclusionary rule and wondered how the rule could be considered so fundamental to a free society if so many free and civilized societies did not hold it so.

Frankfurter recognized, of course, that the Court had applied the exclusionary rule in federal criminal cases, but he stated that this rule was only a Court-created federal rule of evidence and not binding on the states. Frankfurter asked why all the states should be bound with the straitjacket of the federal rule. He concluded that it would be better for each state to act as a laboratory in searching for effective remedies for violations of the Fourth Amendment. He suggested alternative police sanctions to the exclusionary rule, such as suits for money damages, as was the remedy in the famous *Wilkes* case in eighteenth-century England, or criminal and administrative punishments for errant officers.

Justices Douglas, Murphy, and Rutledge dissented. Justice Murphy wrote the sharpest dissenting opinion, challenging Frankfurter's separation of the remedy of exclusion from the Fourth Amendment protection. He restated the language of the Court in *Weeks* that if unlawfully seized evidence can be used against a citizen, "the protection of the Fourth Amendment . . . is of no value, and so far as those placed are concerned, might as well be stricken from the Constitution." Murphy insisted that it was deceptive to speak of alternative remedies to exclusion of evidence. From a practical point of view he wrote, "there is but one alternative remedy to the rule of exclusion. That is no sanction at all."

Justice Murphy scoffed at the alternative remedy of prosecuting the offending officer. He found it unbelievable "to expect a district attorney to prosecute himself or his associates for well-meaning violations of the search and seizure clause during a raid the district attorney or his associates have ordered." As to civil damages against officers in a lawsuit, he found this to be an "illusory remedy." On the one hand, he wrote, it is highly unlikely juries will award damages to criminal defendants against whom the illegally seized evidence was convincing. And on the other hand, he said, even if a criminal defendant were to obtain a substantial verdict, the individual police officer's finances may well make the judgment useless. Justice Murphy found little evidence in the records of successful lawsuits against police officers for violating search and seizure protections.

Eleven years later, Justice Murphy's dissent proved more prophetic of real-life police work than Justice Frankfurter's theoretical majority opinion in *Wolf*. But before that story, we come to a parallel Fourth Amendment adventure involving a far more pervasive and surreptitious invasion of privacy: the story of electronic surveillance—wiretapping and bugging.

CHAPTER 6

The Case of the "Whispering Wires"

I think it less evil that some criminals should escape than that the Government should play an ignoble part . . . if the existing code does not permit district attorneys to have a hand in such dirty business it does not permit the judge to allow such iniquities to succeed.

Justice Oliver Wendell Holmes, dissenting in Olmstead v. United States, 277 U.S. 438, 470 *(1927)*

The time was the Roaring Twenties, years of prosperity in America with a booming economy and a bullish stock market. Jazz, flappers, and the Charleston were sweeping U.S. popular culture. Walt Disney introduced Mickey Mouse. Amelia Earhart won acclaim as the first woman to fly across the Atlantic Ocean. George Gershwin composed "An American in Paris." Elsewhere in the world, Chiang Kai-shek became president of China, Joseph Stalin announced his first five-year plan for the Soviet Union, and Sir Alexander Fleming discovered penicillin.

The high spirits of Americans may have been clouded somewhat by the Eighteenth Amendment to the Constitution in 1919, which brought in the era of Prohibition, but alcohol still flowed in speakeasies and at private social clubs. Liquor was still easy to come by for a price. An organized crime industry supplying bootlegged liquor flourished, protected by police and public officials who shared in the illegal profits. This was the time of hoodlums like Al Capone. Similar to our experience today with efforts to enforce drug laws, federal and local police made many raids and arrested many bootleggers, but the flow of illegal liquor to its willing customers did not seem to stop by even a drop. In charge of the federal enforcement of Prohibition for the state of Washington was Director of Prohibition Roy C. Lyle. On November 17, 1924, Lyle and his agents raided the mansion of Roy Olmstead, a wealthy and prominent citizen of Seattle, Washington, who lived in the exclusive Mount Baker neighborhood of that city.[1] The raiders interrupted a party Olmstead was giving for a number of guests. When the agents entered, the guests were listening to Mrs. Olmstead read bedtime stories during her regular radio program as Aunt Vivien over a radio station broadcasting from the Olmstead home.[2]

Although no evidence of bootlegging was found in the house, Olmstead, his wife, and all of the guests were arrested. Shortly afterward, federal agents rounded up many more members of Olmstead's bootlegging ring, making a total of forty-seven defendants, including two Seattle policemen, charged with violating the federal prohibition law. It was hailed as the biggest criminal prosecution in Washington's history. Director Lyle wanted to destroy the radio station in the Olmstead home, because, he claimed, Mrs. Olmstead was not reading bedtime stories but rather broadcasting coded messages to ships offshore with instructions for bootlegged liquor landings. However, the court ruled that Lyle first had to prove his theory of coded messages, which he never did.[3]

Roy Olmstead had started out as a young patrolman in Seattle. His moxie and connections led to his promotion to the rank of lieutenant.[4] Like many police officers at that time, Olmstead knew where the smart money was in big-city policing. Large bills were literally pouring from the pockets of successful bootleggers, and Olmstead became one of the takers.

Shortly after his promotion, Olmstead was caught in the company of a crew of rumrunners as they received a shipment of liquor.[5] After his arrest, it was learned that Olmstead had given protection to certain bootleggers while providing information about rival operations to local and federal law enforcement authorities. He was first put on probation and then fired from the police department.

Olmstead had already convinced himself that police work was for losers and that the winners were on the other side of the law. With some of his earlier connections, he launched a bootlegging operation that grew so large that he became known as the "King of Bootleggers"—the mastermind of a major criminal organization to import and sell alcohol on the Pacific Coast.[6] Up until the raid on his home in 1924, he had been untouched by the law, having bought protection by payments to police and other public officials. Even after his arrest, he did not worry—no evidence had been found by the raiders.

United States Attorney Thomas P. Revelle had a surprise for Olmstead. Director Lyle and his agents had been wiretapping all of the telephones in the Olmstead home for five months before the raid. In doing so, the agents had violated the criminal law of the state of Washington, which prohibited interception of telephone communications and the use of any evidence obtained by such interception. However, as federal officers, Lyle's agents believed they could ignore state law. The notes the wiretappers took of the overheard incriminating conversations filled 775 typewritten pages. Quickly the press and the lawyers began calling the case "the case of the whispering wires."[7]

The intercepted telephone conversations revealed that Olmstead's criminal organization was as vast as any major industry in the country. It included executives, salesmen, deliverymen, dispatchers, warehousemen, scouts, collectors, and attorneys. He had a fleet of ships that transported alcohol from Scotland to British Columbia and then to speedboats that brought the cargo to hideouts on the Pacific coast of the United States. He also had a fleet of trucks, variously disguised as meat, dairy, or gasoline trucks, to make deliveries to speakeasies and private clubs. This wiretap evidence, if admitted against him at trial, would ensure his conviction.

Olmstead's defense lawyer, Jerry L. Finch, was particularly handicapped. He had been indicted as a co-conspirator in Olmstead's bootlegging operation and was on trial himself.[8] Finch unsuccessfully moved the court for a separate trial, claiming that he represented most of the other defendants, including Olmstead. Nowhere in the record of the trial or in news stories at the time did anyone appear to be concerned over the ethical impropriety of Finch continuing to represent Olmstead while he himself was a defendant in the same trial.

Finch was also unsuccessful on his motion to suppress the wiretap evidence as violating his clients' constitutional rights. Trial judge Jeremiah Netterer ruled that the wiretap evidence was admissible against the defendants despite the fact that the Washington's criminal law had been violated. This was a federal trial, he said, and the proceedings were not bound by state law. Defense lawyer Finch told the jury in his closing argument, before a crowded courtroom with hundreds of spectators crowding outside the court, "If you gentlemen feel the contempt that I do for evidence obtained in such a way, you will not be ten minutes in reaching a verdict."[9] The jury felt otherwise and convicted Olmstead, Finch, and most of the other defendants. Mrs. Olmstead was acquitted. Judge Netterer sentenced Olmstead to four years in federal prison and an eight-thousand-dollar fine. After the sentence was announced, Olmstead surprised everyone in the courtroom by turning to United States Attorney Revelle with a smile, shaking his hand, and congratulating him on doing a good job.[10]

The U.S. Court of Appeals for the Ninth Circuit affirmed the judgment of conviction against Olmstead. The U.S. Supreme Court at first refused to review the case but then reversed itself and agreed to hear it. This was the first criminal conviction based on wiretapping to reach the U.S. Supreme Court. In 1927, when Olmstead's petition for *certiorari* was filed in the court, little was known in the United States about electronic surveillance practices. Washington was only one of a few states that, because of rare exposures, had legislation on the subject.

The single issue before the Supreme Court in *Olmstead* was whether government interception of private telephone communications came within the purview of the Fourth Amendment prohibition against unreasonable searches and seizures. If it did, the court had already ruled in *Weeks* that such evidence would have to be excluded from trial in a federal criminal case. In a five-to-four decision, the majority opinion, written by Chief Justice Taft, held that government wiretap evidence was not obtained by a search and seizure within the coverage of the Fourth Amendment. The chief justice emphasized the fact that the government agents had cut into the telephone wires outside of Olmstead's house and had not trespassed inside the house, as in the case of a traditional search and seizure. Taft also maintained that what was seized by the agents were not tangible things as the wording of the Fourth Amendment required, but intangible words. Finally, Taft concluded that by telephoning their words over wires that stretched everywhere in public, the defendants had voluntarily given their words away for anyone's taking.

The majority did not view the fact that the agents had violated state law in their wiretapping as really relevant. They were satisfied that under the common law, evidence that was relevant and reliable was admissible even though it may have been obtained illegally. Taft also refused to adopt a policy for the court that would permit reversing convictions not because of a constitutional violation but because the government had acted wrongly or unethically in collecting its evidence.

Four justices—Holmes, Brandeis, Butler, and Stone—dissented strongly. The major dissent, joined in by the others, was written by Brandeis. Brandeis scolded the majority for reducing the impact of the Fourth Amendment to the protection only of archaic property rights. Telephone communications, he insisted, are meant to be even more private and confidential than tangible objects. He warned that the sweep of a wiretap reaches many conversations that should never be overheard by government eavesdroppers. Pointing out the anger of the colonists over writs of assistance and general warrants, which exposed mere goods to search and seizure, he said that wiretapping private conversations makes such writs of assistance and general warrants "but puny instruments of tyranny and oppression."

Brandeis reminded the majority that the founders had not intended to draft merely a technical and narrow set of individual protections that applied only to the period of time in which they lived. Brandeis said it was clear that the founders wanted the Constitution to be "immortal." At the time the founders sought to restrict government searches and seizures, the harm they could then envision was forceful intrusion into private homes. Scientific discovery had not advanced to create any greater danger. Brandeis said that the present state of scientific discovery allowed the government to search and seize private information from people in ways unimagined in the eighteenth century.

Accusing the majority of being backward-looking and shortsighted, Brandeis warned that future scientific invention would permit government agents to remove by stealth private papers from secret drawers of a citizen's desk in his home without ever having to enter the home or the desk, and "reproduce them in court . . . to expose to a jury the most intimate occurrences of the home." Computers in homes and offices today have become our modern desks and files, and Brandeis's prophetic vision has come true today with the government's ability to intercept or retrieve computer documents.

Brandeis next gave his support to the dissenting opinion of Justice Holmes, who had called what the agents had done in violating Washington law "dirty business" that should never be permitted to sully the integrity of the courts. Brandeis agreed with Holmes that even if wiretapping were not within the meaning of the Fourth Amendment, the fact that the federal agents had violated the criminal law of Washington State was sufficient reason for the court to exclude the use of the illegally obtained evidence from the trial. With eloquent language that has resounded in courtrooms ever since, Brandeis addressed the ultimate obligation of the government in enforcing the law, saying,

> Decency, security, and liberty alike demand that government officials shall be subjected to the same rules of conduct that are commands to the citizen. In a government of laws, existence of the government will be imperiled if it fails to observe the law scrupulously. Our government is the potent, the omnipresent teacher. For good or for ill, it teaches the whole people by its example. Crime is contagious. If the Government becomes a lawbreaker, it breeds contempt for the law; it invites every man to become a law unto himself; it invites anarchy.

While in prison, Olmstead embraced Christian Science and actively practiced it after his release from prison. He was pardoned by President Franklin D. Roosevelt in 1935. Roosevelt had campaigned on the promise to have Prohibition repealed. An ironic twist in Olmstead's relationship with Director of Prohibition Lyle occurred while Olmstead was still behind bars. The tables had turned on Lyle, an avid Prohibition enforcer. He was now arrested himself and charged with conspiracy in colluding with rumrunners. The temptation of big money appeared to have been too great even for an untouchable. This time, it was Olmstead who was called by the prosecutors to testify against Lyle.[11]

At the time Justice Brandeis was ringing the alarm to awaken the Supreme Court to the dangers of wiretapping, he, the Court, and the rest of the country were oblivious to the pervasive and overwhelming practices of electronic surveillance in the United States by law enforcement agencies and private individuals and businesses. What is more, these practices had been the hidden underbelly of investigations for many years. Interception of electronic communications began with the introduction of electronic communication in this country. That was the telegraph in the mid-nineteenth century.

In the 1850s, the first telegraph poles were erected in the eastern part of the United States, and their wires began to stretch westward as the country expanded. There is evidence that the first telegraph pole erected was climbed by the first wiretapper. As early as 1862, California found it necessary to enact legislation prohibiting the interception of telegraph messages.[12] One of the first wiretappers prosecuted under this act was a former stockbroker who was arrested in 1864 for masterminding a conspiracy to intercept news of stock operations coming from the East and to sell this information to certain subscribers.[13]

During the Civil War, military telegraph messages were being intercepted by both sides of the conflict. Confederate General Jeb Stuart actually had his own personal wiretapper travel with him in the field.[14] After the Civil War, a number of former telegraph operators engaged in wiretapping as a private business. A Boston newspaper reporter who had been a Civil War telegrapher was reported to have often saved himself the trouble of newsgathering by wiretapping the dispatches of other correspondents as they were sent over the wires.

In 1876, a congressional committee investigating Washington, D.C., real estate dealings pounced upon three-quarters of a ton of telegraph messages collected in one of the offices of the Atlantic and Pacific Tea Company. The *New York Times* of June 24, 1876, reflected the public's outrage:

> These messages relate to the private business affairs of a great many people. . . . Here is the telegraph correspondence of unaccused and unoffending citizens hauled about and thumbed by a knot of gossips. These persons, Democratic congressmen and clerks, when they have read, arranged, digested, and indexed these messages, may turn out to be blackmailers or the accessories of blackmailers. The whole proceeding is an outrage upon the liberties of the citizen which no plea of public necessity can justify.

The beginnings of telephone wiretapping occurred in the early and middle 1890s. Alexander Bell had introduced the telephone in 1876 at the Centennial Exposition in Philadelphia. In 1878, the first switchboard for commercial service was put into operation in New Haven,

Connecticut, with twenty-one subscribers. By the early 1890s, when telephone wiretapping was in its early infancy, there were only 339,500 telephones in the entire country, representing 0.48 telephones per 100 Americans.

As had been the case in telegraph wiretapping, rival newspapers began intercepting their competitors' telephone calls to pick up "scoops." This practice existed across the country. It was reported in Boston, New York, Chicago, and San Francisco. In 1895, Illinois enacted legislation prohibiting wiretapping for the purpose of intercepting news dispatches. A sensational wiretapping scandal broke in San Francisco in 1899. The *San Francisco Call* hired the Pinkerton Detective Agency to investigate how the *San Francisco Examiner* was able to report the *Call's* exclusive stories on the same day the *Call* exposed them. The Pinkerton detectives discovered that an *Examiner* reporter was wiretapping the *Call's* telephones.

The *Call* denounced this intrusion on its front page.[15] Covering the entire left side of the page was a drawing of a beautiful woman talking into the mouthpiece of an antique telephone. The drawing of a coiled wire from that telephone stretched across the top of the page to another antique telephone drawn on the right side of the page. A drawing of a well-dressed man in a bowler hat holding the receiver of the telephone covered the entire right side of the page. Intersecting the wire at the center of the top of the page was the drawing of another wire, which descended down the middle of the page to the bottom, where there was the drawing of an evil-looking man with a handlebar moustache sitting in front of a rolltop desk holding an earpiece listening in to the conversation.

A speech balloon drawn from the mouth of the man on the right side of the page contained the words, "I must work tonight, honey." The speech balloon from the woman's mouth replies, "Please don't work too late, darling." The text of the *Call's* story begins, "In these modern times the fact that our most precious secrets are at the mercy of eavesdroppers who invade our privacy is outrageous and must be prohibited by law."[16] It took until 1905 for the *San Francisco Call* to get the California legislature to extend its 1862 prohibition against telegraph wiretapping to telephone wiretapping.

Telephone wiretapping by the police in criminal investigations also began during the infancy of telephone communications. New York police were actively using wiretapping in their investigations in 1895. A loose arrangement existed between the New York Police Department and the telephone company whereby the telephone company cooperated with police wiretapping.[17] In 1916, it was revealed that the mayor of New York had authorized the New York police to wiretap the telephone conversations of five Catholic priests to obtain evidence for a special New York Commission investigating charity fraud.[18] The charges against the priests were dismissed, and the police wiretappers were prosecuted but were exonerated when the court found nothing illegal about police wiretapping.

The wiretapping of the priests' conversations led to a New York legislative investigation of police wiretapping. The legislative committee learned that police had been wiretapping since 1895 and had the means to listen in to any telephone conversation in the entire New York telephone system with the cooperation of the telephone company. Police witnesses testified that they listened in on many telephone conversations, including conversations of lawyers and physicians. When a legislator asked a police sergeant, "If you overheard a confidential communication of a client to his lawyer, you wouldn't tell your superiors about it, would you?" The officer replied, "I would not."[19]

There were similar exposures during World War I and leading up to the wide use of wiretapping to enforce Prohibition. Yet this history appears to have been forgotten at the time the Supreme Court held in *Olmstead* that wiretapping was not a search and seizure under the Fourth Amendment. Nowhere in the briefs of the petitioners before the Supreme Court was any mention made of the documented police practices that proved that wiretapping was used pervasively in the United States to invade the private communications of the people. This history was also not referred to in the majority or dissenting opinions. Brandeis, particularly, excelled in bolstering his arguments with factual history and would have been expected to draw on the wide-sweeping wiretapping practices of the police since the 1890s to support his dissent if he had known about them.

Congress was surprised and shocked by the Supreme Court's ruling in *Olmstead*. Congressmen and senators were among those most fearful of electronic surveillance, particularly of their political communications. The year after the Court's ruling, a bill was introduced in Congress to prohibit the admission of evidence gained by wiretapping, but it failed to become law. In 1932, similar bills fell short of passage. Finally, in 1934, Congress enacted the Federal Communications Act, which prohibited, in §605, all interception of radio or wire communications and the divulgence of the contents of such communications, except by the consent of the sender.[20] The "sender" was interpreted as covering all parties to the communications, who were, in turn, senders and receivers.

This statute effectively wiped out the impact of *Olmstead* in both federal and state wiretapping, although it could not affect the court's constitutional interpretation of the Fourth Amendment. New York, in 1938, tried to give its law enforcement officers the right to wiretap under a court order through a state constitutional amendment,[21] but the Supreme Court ruled that the Federal Communications Act prohibition was the supreme law of the land and states could not exempt themselves from its coverage.[22]

Nevertheless, Congress had left a gaping hole in the statute that permitted a form of electronic surveillance as pervasive as wiretapping. It did not cover, and perhaps jurisdictionally could not have covered, surreptitious overhearing or recording by microphone of private oral communications in homes, offices, or other private places. This form of eavesdropping, called "bugging," was as widely used as telephone wire-tapping by state and federal law enforcement officers and by private parties. Part of the reason bugging went unregulated was that the electronic surveillance scandals that were publicized involved only telephone wiretapping. Yet secret recording or listening in to private oral communications by microphone had been a pervasive practice also since the late nineteenth century.

It was not until 1942 that the issue of "bugging" came before the Supreme Court. In *Goldman v. United States*,[23] FBI agents were able to hear the suspect's conversations through the other side of his office wall. They used what was called a detectaphone, a microphone with a suction cup that was attached to the wall of the room adjoining the suspect's office. The sound waves caused by the suspect's voice bounced off the inner wall of his room and could be detected by the sensitive microphone suctioned onto the wall of the agents' room.

Goldman moved to suppress the overheard conversations on the ground that they had been obtained by an unlawful search and seizure in violation of the Fourth Amendment. The Supreme Court ruled against him, reasoning that since there had been no physical invasion or trespass of Goldman's room nor any seizure of tangible things, only abstract words, no violation of the Fourth Amendment had occurred. Also, the agents had not violated the prohibition of the Federal Communications Act, because they had not intercepted any radio or wire communications, only oral communications.[24]

While §605 of the Federal Communications Act prohibited interception of radio communications, there was no violation if the interception was consented to by one of the parties to the conversation. The value of this exception was confirmed for law enforcement surveillance by the Supreme Court when it approved the use as evidence of an intercepted incriminating conversation obtained by a federal agent listening through a radio receiver to a conversation between an informer, wearing a hidden small radio transmitter, and a suspect in his laundry shop.[25]

By the time of the trial, the informer had disappeared and the only witness was the federal agent, who testified to what he heard over his earphones. The Supreme Court upheld the conviction based on this testimony on the ground that the informer, who was a party to the conversation, had consented to the agent listening in to the broadcast words. With the informer not available, if he existed at all, the integrity of the conviction had to rest on the credibility of the federal agent. The convicted defendant believed he had a good chance to obtain a new trial when he learned that the federal agent who had testified he overheard the conversation was fired by the government for committing perjury in another case. Despite this new information, the U.S. Court of Appeals for the Second Circuit refused to reopen the case.[26]

In the midst of this ambiguity and conflicting signals over electronic surveillance practices, as well as because of the general unawareness in the country of the nature and extent of these practices, the Fund for the Republic, an offshoot of the Ford Foundation, in 1957 gave a grant to the Pennsylvania Bar Foundation for a nationwide study of electronic surveillance. After two years of often-undercover investigation of both law enforcement and private electronic surveillance, the grant investigator published his report in a book titled *The Eavesdroppers*.[27]

The book publicly disclosed for the first time the history of electronic surveillance, with a detailed description of wiretapping and bugging practices by police in several representative states. It also revealed the hitherto unknown story of pervasive private wiretapping in every aspect of life in the United States. For example, it reported on how business executives of major companies electronically eavesdropped on their employees through microphones hidden in the walls of the men's and ladies' rest rooms and in their desks and through wiretaps on their office telephones.[28] Many of these same companies hired the services of wiretappers to listen in to their competitors' telephones and offices. This was especially true in the cosmetic industry. The telephone company bugged the pen sets of their operators to, as they claimed, check on the courteousness of the operators.[29] Some restaurants bugged the centerpiece on the tables, allegedly for the same reason.[30] Some model homes were similarly equipped with hidden microphones to allow salespersons to overhear what prospective buyers said about the size of closets or the kitchen design.

More morbidly, some salesmen in showrooms for coffins even placed microphones in the coffin linings to sample comments of bereaved customers. The same practice was used by automobile salesmen, who placed microphones in the closing rooms.[31] When a husband and wife were hesitant in closing the deal, the salesman would excuse himself and go to a listening post to overhear what was troubling his customers. Then he was able to come back and resolve the sale by offering what they had quietly said to each other they wanted.

Private electronic surveillance was most active in domestic relations battles. Husbands bugged their wives' bedrooms and wiretapped their home telephones while wives wiretapped and bugged their husbands' offices.

The Eavesdroppers also disclosed the wide-scale use of wiretapping and bugging by police and the kinds of equipment they used in every jurisdiction of the country. Even in 1959, the electronic eavesdropping devices had been designed to escape discovery. Some were disguised as tiepins or earrings. In one instance, officers worked a small transmitter into the shoulder padding of a suspect's suit jacket while it was at the cleaners. Flat, paper-thin broadcasting transmitters were inserted in the backs of diplomas or pictures on office walls and remained hidden there for years. A parabolic microphone could be aimed at the open window of an office and pick up conversations inside the office as far as one thousand feet away. Citing *The Eavesdroppers*, Justice Stewart called these devices "frightening paraphernalia."[32] The findings of the study were reported to Congress in a number of hearings, which were widely publicized.

Perhaps the most disturbing revelation in *The Eavesdroppers* was the finding that recorded intercepted conversations could be readily edited through electronic equipment.[33] In an experiment conducted by the investigator, a statement that expressed love for parents and country and commitment to honesty and morality was recorded on tape. The tape was given to a New York broadcasting station technician with the instructions to edit the tape by changing the message into one that confessed to killing an FBI agent and conspiring to overthrow the government by force and violence.

In a short time, the technician had completed the transformation of the taped message. No new words had been recorded on the tape. The technician had slowed down the speed of the tape and had rearranged syllables and consonants to fabricate new words that had not been spoken in the original message. For example, the word "kill" had not been spoken in the original statement. The technician was able to remove the "k" sound from the word "kindled" and transfer it to the word "fill" after removing the "f" sound from "fill," leaving "ill." Thus, the new word "kill" was created in the same voice sound of the investigator. The edited spliced tape was recorded on a clean tape, and the editing could not be detected by the use of sophisticated electronic instruments at the Moore School of Electrical Engineering of the University of Pennsylvania.[34]

During this period of heightened awareness of electronic surveillance practices, another FBI bugging case came before the Supreme Court in 1961. The facts duplicated those in the *Goldman* case. This time, the agents gained permission to occupy a vacant house adjoining the house of their suspect, Julius Silverman. Relying on their success in *Goldman*, the FBI placed a microphone on the wall of a second-floor room of the house they were occupying to capture the conversations of the suspect in the adjoining house. However, this time, to obtain better sound, the agents used a "spike mike," which was a microphone with a thin, foot-long spike attached to it. They inserted the spike in a crevice under the floor baseboard of their room and pushed it into the space between the houses until it hit something solid, which turned out to be the heating duct that serviced the suspect's house. Once the spike touched the heating duct, the duct became a giant microphone running through the entire house occupied by the suspect. The FBI agents were able, through their earphones, to hear all of the suspect's conversations on both floors of his house.

The noted criminal defense lawyer Edward Bennett Williams represented Silverman. He attached as an appendix to his brief a copy of *The Eavesdroppers.* He argued that the new exposures of electronic surveillance practices and devices required the Court to reconsider its prior decisions holding that wiretapping and bugging were not covered by the Fourth Amendment. Justice Stewart, writing for the Court, said that the Court did not in this case "have to contemplate the Fourth Amendment implications of these and other frightening paraphernalia [described in *The Eavesdroppers*] which the vaunted marvels of an electronic age may visit upon human society." The Court ruled that the conviction must be reversed because the agents had, in fact, trespassed into the private areas of Silverman's house by use of the spike mike. This fact, according to the Court, distinguished this case from *Olmstead* and *Goldman* and made the agents' conduct an unlawful search and seizure in violation of the Fourth Amendment. Also, the Court now held that "words" are "things" under the Fourth Amendment, contrary to their position in *Olmstead*.[35]

The Supreme Court's insistence that the Fourth Amendment protection applied only when law enforcement officers made a physical trespass in a private area was now earmarked for reversal after *Silverman*. In a practical sense, this reversal occurred shortly after *Silverman*, when the government agents secured their microphone on their wall by a thumbtack, which did not intrude at all into the wall space between the agents' room and suspect's room. Yet, without further explanation, the Supreme Court reversed the conviction, citing *Silverman*.

A few years later, in 1967, the Supreme Court specifically overruled its decisions in *Olmstead* and *Goldman*. FBI agents had been observing a man named Katz, who they suspected of operating an illegal interstate number-running operation based on horse racing, use a particular telephone booth on a regular basis. They decided to listen in on one of his telephone calls from the booth.

The agents knew that they were prohibited from wiretapping the telephone under the Federal Communications Act. They also knew from the Supreme Court's decisions in *Goldman* and *Silverman* that whatever listening device they used, they had to be careful not to intrude into the inside space of the telephone booth. So they adopted the strategy used by the agents in *Goldman* and attached to the roof of the telephone booth a suction microphone, which had no protruding parts that could enter any protected space in the booth. The microphone allowed them to hear what Katz said on the telephone but not what was said by the other party to the call.

The agents waited until Katz entered the telephone booth and closed the door to start listening in. What they heard Katz say persuaded them that Katz had made a long-distance call to Florida and was receiving racing news. The agents arrested Katz and charged him with violating federal interstate gambling laws. Katz was convicted at trial, and his conviction was upheld by the U.S. Circuit Court of Appeals on the ground that under the Supreme Court's ruling in *Goldman*, there had been no Fourth Amendment violation by the agents because they had made no physical penetration into the booth.

The Supreme Court agreed to review the case and reversed Katz's conviction by a vote of seven to one, Justice Marshall not participating in the case.[36] Justice Black dissented. Writing for the Court, Justice

Stewart made a clean break from *Olmstead* and *Goldman*, rejecting them as out of date with modern technology and not within the spirit of the Fourth Amendment. He stated that the Court's Fourth Amendment law should no longer be entangled with such irrelevant property concepts as "physical trespass" or "constitutionally protected space." The Fourth Amendment protects people, not property, Stewart insisted. In *Katz*, Stewart said the question was whether the agents had violated Katz's effort to preserve his conversation as private, "even in an area accessible to the public." It was not relevant where the electronic listening device had been placed, he said, but only whether the device permitted the agents to listen in to a conversation that Katz sought to keep private. The court held that Katz had done so when he used a telephone booth to make a telephone call. To the government's argument that the telephone booth had a glass door and gave Katz no privacy from the passing public, Stewart replied that when Katz closed the door to the booth, it was for the purpose of keeping out the uninvited ear, not the uninvited eye.

With electronic surveillance now placed squarely within the coverage of the Fourth Amendment, the Court made it clear that reasonable searches through such means could be made in compliance with Fourth Amendment standards where the officers had probable cause and obtained prior judicial approval through a court order or warrant.

The Supreme Court's ruling in *Katz* prompted the Congress the following year, in 1968, to enact a statute that regulated and authorized law enforcement wiretapping and bugging under the same standards that governed reasonable searches and seizures. Title III of the Safe Streets Act of 1968[37] imposed probable cause and court order requirements on government electronic surveillance. In addition, it contained a number of restrictive limitations on this kind of surreptitious and pervasive search and seizure based on the disclosures of *The Eavesdroppers* in a number of congressional hearings.

For example, the statute limited the time of wiretapping or bugging to thirty days but required the officers to stop listening or recording as soon as they obtained the information authorized to be intercepted in the court order, even if they obtained it at the very beginning of the surveillance. This limitation reflected the recognition by Congress that the very nature of private telephone conversations would expose many innocent conversations to government eavesdroppers unless strict limitations were imposed.

For the same reason, the statute mandated that the court order impose on the officers the requirement to "minimize" their intrusion in private communications. This meant that as soon as it became apparent to the officer listening in that the conversation was innocent and not related to the criminal information sought, the officer must stop listening. Otherwise, the draftsmen and some members of the Supreme Court believed, court-ordered electronic surveillance of private conversations would, in effect, become a dragnet search like those under the hated general warrants the American colonialists resisted and the drafters of the Fourth Amendment sought to prohibit.

However, this reasonable restriction was nullified by the Supreme Court when it agreed with the argument of the Department of Justice that it was not a violation of the minimization requirement of the statute if an agent who listened in to every conversation, even those apparently innocent, did so believing that the so-called innocent words were really coded messages in pursuance of the criminal enterprise. Thus, in a case where the agents listened in to all the calls (80 percent of which appeared to be innocent), including ones like the wife's call to a butcher to order two pounds of lamb chops, the court found no statute violation because it found the government's argument reasonable that the calls could have been, in reality, coded calls to conspirators concerning illegal drug transactions.[38] Under this reasoning, the minimization restriction in the statute becomes meaningless.

Congress also responded to the revelation in *The Eavesdroppers* of the danger of undetectable editing of recorded communications. They provided in the new statute a safeguard provision against editing. This provision required the officer to deliver the original tape to the clerk of the court for identification and sealing as soon as the wiretap or bugging was complete. When the recording needed to be introduced as evidence at trial, the court custodian would deliver the tape and certify to the continuous chain of custody of the sealed tape, which had prevented any attempt at altering it.

Since the passage of the 1968 statute, technology, of course, has continued to advance and outpace the coverage of the statute. For example, the development of computer technology has introduced completely new ways for people to communicate locally, nationally, and internationally. E-mail has replaced, to a large extent, the telephone and the mailed letter. Belatedly, Congress amended the Safe Streets Act to reflect this new technology and to impose similar safeguards against interception of this new form of communication. Similarly, tagging and tracing devices to allow police to keep suspects under surveillance have required amendments to the statute.

As in any war, the crime warriors have discovered that their latest developed technology to detect and solve crime has been countered by defensive technology developed by their targets. Most recently, businesses and organized crime groups have transformed their communications into code through encryption or by the use of scrambling devices. The FBI has waged a successful campaign under the inapt name "Carnivore" to gain access to these codes under circumstances restricted to criminal investigations.

In the meantime, while the Supreme Court and Congress were bringing electronic surveillance under the Fourth Amendment, the question of what sanctions should be imposed in the states for unlawful searches and seizures was still being debated. As we have seen, the

Supreme Court sought to resolve that question in *Wolf v. Colorado*[39] when it ruled that the Fourteenth Amendment guarantee of due process for criminal defendants in state cases did not require the states to adopt the federal exclusionary rule mandated by the *Weeks* decision. Indeed, even after Congress outlawed wiretapping in the Federal Communications Act, the Supreme Court ruled that evidence obtained by illegal wiretapping was still permitted to be used against a defendant in state courts.[40] However, this question of sanction, so crucial to the enforcement of the Fourth Amendment, ripened again, in 1961, in a case brought to the Supreme Court by an Ohio woman named Dolly Mapp.

CHAPTER 7

Dolly Mapp

The criminal goes free, if he must, but it is the law that sets him free. Nothing can destroy a government more quickly than its failure to observe its own laws, or worse, its disregard of the charter of its own existence.

Justice Tom C. Clark, Mapp v. Ohio, 367 U.S. 643
(1961)

Dollree Mapp, also known as Dolly, was an African American woman who lived alone with her twelve-year-old daughter on the second floor of a two-story brick house in the Shaker Heights section of Cleveland, Ohio. Shaker Heights was one of the earliest successfully integrated communities in which blacks and whites lived harmoniously together. Mapp made extra money by subletting other rooms in the house.

She was divorced from heavyweight boxer Jimmy Bivens. In 1956, Mapp claimed that heavyweight boxing championship contender Archie Moore jilted her. She was twenty-eight at the time and was described by those who knew her as a "head turner." She filed a lawsuit against Moore, charging him with breach of promise to marry her and raping her minor daughter. The suit was filed in Chicago, where, at the time, Moore was training for his championship fight against Floyd Patterson. A federal district court judge threw Mapp's suit out on jurisdictional grounds because neither Mapp nor Moore resided in Chicago.[1] One year later, Mapp was involved in more serious trouble.

On May 23, 1957, a bomb blast splintered numbers racketeer Don King's[2] house in Cleveland. Sergeant Carl Delau of the Cleveland police vice squad sped to the scene. King told Delau, "Shondor Birns did this." According to King, crime syndicate figure Shondor Birns was demanding cash payoffs from King for letting King run a numbers game. King had fallen behind in the payments, and the bomb was a noisy reminder.[3] Sergeant Delau set out with two partners to find Birns and "put the squeeze" on him.

During his rounds, Delau spotted a car he knew belonged to a numbers gambler who might lead him to Birns. The car was parked in the driveway of a house on Milverton Road where Delau knew Dollree Mapp lived. Delau knew that Mapp worked the edges of the numbers racket, picking up and delivering betting slips.[4] Delau and his partner banged on the side door, which was the entrance to Mapp's second-floor apartment. "Let me in, Dollree," he called out. She looked out the window and asked what they wanted. Delau said they wanted to talk to her about something and again asked her to let them in. Mapp told the officers that she was going to call her lawyer first. She then came back to the window and informed the officers that her lawyer told her not to let the police enter without showing her a search warrant.

"We didn't have a warrant," Delau later told a reporter. "We make hundreds of searches of houses a year and use a warrant maybe only two times. We didn't think we needed one."[5] But stopped by Mapp's insistence on a warrant, Delau called his superior officer, and later the three officers were joined by four others, one of them carrying a piece of paper. Delau took the piece of paper, which later he described as a simple affidavit and not a court-approved warrant, and broke into the house through the rear door.

Mapp was on the stair landing to the second floor when she saw the police officers in the hall. She again asked if they had a search warrant. Sergeant Delau waved the paper in front of her. She grabbed it and put it in the bosom of her blouse. Delau reached with his hand into her blouse and retrieved the paper. She never had a chance to read it, and by the time of her trial, it had disappeared.

Angry at Mapp's resistance, Delau twisted Mapp's arms behind her and handcuffed her, causing her to cry out that it hurt her. The officers forced her to her bedroom, where they made a wide search of her bureau, desk, closet, and personal effects. The search spread to other rooms in the apartment, including her daughter's room. They also went to the basement and searched through a trunk and some boxes. All that this sweeping search produced were some pornographic pictures and four books—*Affairs of a Troubadour, Little Darlings, London Stage Affairs,* and *Memories of a Hotel Man.* Mapp was arrested and taken to the police station where she was charged with violating Ohio's obscenity law.

Mapp's lawyer filed a motion to suppress the books and pictures on the ground that there had been no valid search warrant authorizing their seizure. The trial court denied the motion. Mapp's defense on the obscenity charge was that the seized material did not belong to her. She said that they belonged to a tenant who had left and was not returning. She had packed up his things, including the pictures and books, and stored them in a trunk in the basement. The trial judge charged the jury that even if what Mapp said was true, they could still find she "possessed" the obscene materials in violation of the law because she still had control over them. The jury convicted Mapp and she was sentenced by the court to imprisonment in the Ohio Reformatory for Women for an indeterminate period of two to seven years.

The Ohio Supreme Court to which Mapp appealed agreed that the search and seizure had taken place without a warrant in violation of Ohio law. However, relying on the U.S. Supreme Court's decision in *Wolf v. Colorado,* the Ohio court affirmed the conviction and said that the U.S. Supreme Court had permitted each state to apply its own rule of evidence on whether illegally seized evidence should be excluded, and the rule in Ohio did not exclude such evidence. The Ohio Supreme Court took notice, however, of the evidence in the record of the brutal manner in which the police officers treated Mapp. The court suggested that this abusive conduct might alone have required a reversal of the conviction if the evidence had been seized from her own person through such police misconduct. But the court concluded that the evidence taken from her home was seized not from her person but from searches of various places in the home.

Although four of the seven justices of the Ohio Supreme Court held that the Ohio obscenity statute was unconstitutional, a simple majority was not enough under the Ohio Constitution to invalidate the statute on constitutional grounds, and so the court affirmed her conviction. Mapp appealed the Ohio Supreme Court's ruling to the U.S. Supreme Court under that Court's jurisdiction to review state statutes that are claimed to be unconstitutional under the U.S. Constitution. What happened in that appeal is one of the most surprising and controversial stories in Supreme Court history.

By a vote of six to three, the U.S. Supreme Court overruled the judgment of the Ohio Supreme Court and reversed Mapp's conviction and set her free. That much is clear. Why and how the Court freed Dollree Mapp is what caused an Olympic furor among the justices. Justice Potter Stewart, after retiring from the Court, told the story in a series of lectures at Columbia Law School.[6] He said that when the Court met in conference after the oral arguments in Mapp to decide the case, most of the justices voted to reverse the conviction on the ground that the Ohio obscenity statute was unconstitutional. Stewart recalled that neither the exclusionary rule nor the question of reconsidering Wolf v. Colorado was even discussed by the justices.

Justice Tom C. Clark was assigned to write the opinion for the Court, and according to Justice Stewart, he and most of the other justices expected it to be an opinion on the unconstitutionality of the Ohio obscenity law. To Stewart's shock, the draft opinion Justice Clark circulated was not based on the Ohio obscenity statute at all, but was an opinion overruling *Wolf v. Colorado* and holding that the rule of exclusion of illegally seized evidence applied to the states as an integral part of the Fourth Amendment and the due process clause of the Fourteenth Amendment.

Justice Stewart told his audience at Columbia that he angrily sent a memo to Justice Clark complaining that such a historically significant ruling on the exclusionary rule should not have been written in the absence of full briefing and oral argument by counsel and full discussion by the justices. Rather than join this "outlaw" opinion, but still believing the conviction should be reversed, Stewart concurred in a separate memorandum supporting the reversal, but solely on the ground that the Ohio statute was unconstitutional.[7] Speculating on how Clark's opinion developed, Stewart said that he believes a rump private meeting of the justices favoring overruling *Wolf v. Colorado* was held in Clark's chambers, which led to Clark's decision to write the opinion. These justices would have been Chief Justice Warren and Justices Douglas, Brennan, and Black.

Justice Harlan, one of the most skillful lawyers on the Court, was furious. He wrote a blistering dissent that accused the majority of forgetting "the sense of judicial restraint which, with due regard to *stare decisis*, is one element that should enter into deciding whether a past decision of this Court should be overruled." Harlan complained that reconsideration of the *Wolf* decision was not properly before the Court. He stated that the principal issue decided by the Ohio Supreme Court and which was tendered by appellant's jurisdictional statement and briefed and argued before the Court was the constitutionality of the Ohio obscenity statute. "In this posture of things," Harlan complained, "I think it fair to say five members of this Court simply 'reached out' to overrule *Wolf*."

In language unmatched for its harshness against brethren justices, except for the more recent dissent in *Bush v. Gore*, Harlan closed with the declaration, "But in the last analysis I think this Court can increase respect for the Constitution only if it rigidly respects the limitations which the Constitution places upon it, and respects as well the principles inherent in its own process. In the present case I think we exceed both, and that our voice becomes only a voice of power, not of reason."

How fair were these accusations of Stewart and Harlan? Doubtless, the Court took up Mapp's appeal for the sole purpose of reviewing the constitutionality of the Ohio obscenity statute. But Stewart and Harlan were wrong in claiming that the Ohio Supreme Court did not decide the issue of the admissibility of the illegally seized evidence in the state criminal case or rely on *Wolf v. Colorado*. The Ohio court specifically held the evidence admissible in Ohio and cited the *Wolf* ruling in support of its holding.

Mapp's lawyer did not raise that issue on appeal. Only the American Civil Liberties Union in their *amicus curiae* brief raised the issue of overruling *Wolf*. Even though in his jurisdictional statement presented to the Court Mapp's lawyer complained about the warrantless search, he did not request the Court to reconsider its ruling in *Wolf v. Colorado*. This was also true in the lawyer's brief and oral argument. He devoted substantial time to describing the unlawful search of Mapp's house and the brutal manner in which it was conducted, but when one of the justices asked him if he was arguing that the Court should overrule the *Wolf* decision, he replied, "No." Harlan, in his dissent, pointed out that Mapp's lawyer even candidly admitted he did not know about the *Wolf* case.

So, on procedural grounds, Stewart and Harlan correctly took the Mapp majority to task. Though their noses were justly out of joint, the substantive merits of what happened surely are in Justice Clark's favor. Justice Harlan's procedural complaint rested on what he called "a summary reversal of *Wolf* without argument." He wrote that he unsuccessfully tried to get the majority to wait until another case was properly before the Court for the reconsideration of the *Wolf* decision, or to, at least, order reargument of the *Mapp* case to permit full briefing, oral arguments, and Court discussion on the issue of whether *Wolf* should be overruled.

But what more could be argued to change the majority's strong and persuasive position rejecting the *Wolf* decision? This was not a case where some justices deceptively and improperly distorted the law to impose a political or ideological point of view. Justice Clark was a conservative on the Court and had a tough law-and-order background as attorney general of the United States. Rather, it seems clear what happened. While it is true that the case was presented to the Court on the fairly uncomplicated issue of the constitutionality of so vague and broad an obscenity law as the Ohio statute, the record of the facts of the case read by the justices was replete with the account of the arbitrary and lawless conduct of the Cleveland police in manhandling Mapp and in searching her house.

Chief Justice Warren, and certainly Justices Clark and Brennan, must have been outraged that, unlike federal police, state police could arrogantly violate the law this way and smugly believe that no one could do anything about it—that under *Wolf*, the evidence would be admitted anyway. *Wolf* now made no sense to them. Why should it be that on one side of the street the federal prosecutor could not use such illegally seized evidence, yet on the other side the state prosecutor could?

Had not the Court just struck down the invidious practice whereby state police, having illegally seized evidence, would hand it over to the federal prosecutor who had been permitted to use it because no federal officer had acted unlawfully? Conversely, federal officers who had seized evidence unlawfully knew that they could hand this evidence over to state prosecutors who could use it to obtain state convictions. This practice was pointedly called the "silver platter" doctrine. But in *Elkins v. United States*, decided only the year before *Mapp* was argued, the Court rejected this absurd doctrine and held that federal agents could not use illegally obtained evidence even if they themselves had not participated in any unlawful conduct. Justice Clark believed that the natural consequence from this decision was to require state prosecutions to be constitutionally restricted with regard to illegal searches and seizures in the same way and by the same remedy applicable to federal prosecutions.

"This makes good sense," Justice Clark wrote in his opinion in *Mapp*. He went on to say,

> There is no war between the Constitution and common sense. Presently a federal prosecutor may make no use of evidence illegally seized, but a State's attorney across the street may, although he supposedly is operating under the enforcement prohibitions of the same Amendment. Thus the State, by admitting evidence unlawfully seized, serves to encourage disobedience of the Federal Constitution which it is bound to uphold.

How could Justice Clark and the others who joined him ignore this blatant inconsistency of constitutional law enforcement that confronted them in the *Mapp* record? This was the time and the occasion to set the law straight and to walk away from *Wolf v. Colorado*. But to do so, Justice Clark first had to dismantle the support structure Justice Frankfurter had built in *Wolf*.

As earlier shown, Justice Frankfurter premised his opinion in *Wolf* on the ground that the exclusionary rule mandated in the *Weeks* case in federal cases was not a fundamental requirement of the Fourth Amendment, but was merely a federal rule of evidence, a federal remedy, that state courts could ignore. Justice Clark quickly rejected this position in his opinion. "There are in the cases of this Court," he wrote, "some passing references to the *Weeks* rule as being one of evidence. But the plain and unequivocal language of *Weeks*—and its later paraphrase in *Wolf*—to the effect that the *Weeks* rule is of constitutional origin, remains entirely undisturbed."

Justice Frankfurter's conclusion that the exclusionary rule was not an integral part of the Fourth Amendment was based on his presumption that there were alternative remedies to exclusion that could be just as effective, and thus the exclusionary rule was not necessary to make the Fourth Amendment effective. Justice Clark held that this factual discussion of alternative remedies was irrelevant to the question of whether the exclusionary rule was mandated by the Fourth Amendment. Nevertheless, he demonstrated that, in fact, the so-called alternative remedies had been shown to be "worthless and futile." Justice Clark concluded,

> It, therefore, plainly appears that the factual considerations supporting the failure of the *Wolf* Court to include the *Weeks* exclusionary rule when it recognized the enforceability of the right to privacy against the States in 1949, while not basically relevant to the constitutional consideration, could not, in any analysis, now be deemed controlling.

Thus, Justice Clark held that the exclusionary rule was an integral part of the Fourth Amendment. Otherwise, he said, as the Court said in *Weeks*, the Fourth Amendment would be mere words on paper and might as well be stricken from the Constitution. Justice Clark said that time had set its face against the premises of the *Wolf* decision. "We hold," he stated, "that all evidence obtained by searches and seizures in violation of the Constitution is, by that same authority, inadmissible in a State court."

Justice Clark also directly challenged Justice Cardozo's often repeated sarcasm—"The criminal is to go free because the constable has blundered." He now answered Justice Cardozo:

> In some cases this will undoubtedly be the result. But . . . there is another consideration—the imperative of judicial integrity. . . . The criminal goes free, if he must, but it is the law that sets him free. Nothing can destroy a government more quickly than its failure to observe its own laws, or worse, its disregard of the charter of its own existence.

Justice Clark's lofty and concluding language in his opinion holding that the exclusionary rule is a necessary and integral part of the Fourth Amendment right of privacy bears emphasizing. This is so because, as we shall see, the post–Warren Court repeatedly forgot or misrepresented this language in its later cases, eroding the exclusionary rule and the Fourth Amendment. Though it was repetitive, Justice Clark once more declared:

> The ignoble shortcut to conviction left open to the States tends to destroy the entire system of constitutional restraints on which the liberties of the people rest. Having once recognized that the right to privacy embodied in the Fourth Amendment is enforceable against the States, and that the right to be secure against rude invasions of privacy by State officers is, therefore, constitutional in origin, we can no longer permit that right to remain an empty promise. Because it is enforceable in the same manner and to like effect as other basic rights secured by the Due Process Clause, we can no longer permit it to be revocable at the whim of any police officer who, in the name of law enforcement, itself, chooses to suspend its enjoyment. Our decision, founded on reason and truth, gives to the individual no more than that which the constitution guarantees him, to the police officer no less than that to which honest law enforcement is entitled, and, to the courts, the judicial integrity so necessary in the true administration of justice.

What arguments later presented to the Court could Justice Harlan believe would rob Justice Clark's opinion of its basic validity? Justice Harlan tried to make these arguments himself in his dissent when he sought to defend the Court's prior ruling in *Wolf*. He repeated Justice Frankfurter's distinction between the fundamental due process right of privacy, inherent in the Fourth Amendment applicable to the states, and the remedy of exclusion for violation of that right which was not fundamental under due process, and therefore not applicable to the states. Justice Harlan argued that this distinction held true even if Justice Clark was right that alternative remedies to the exclusionary rule were worthless.

Thus, as Justice Clark complained of Frankfurter's opinion in *Wolf*, Justice Harlan was holding out the promise of privacy to state citizens regarding state police conduct toward them while denying them the realization of that precious right. Justice Harlan's defense of *Wolf* simply failed to resolve Justice Day's concern in *Weeks* and Justice Clark's in *Mapp*, that without the exclusionary rule the Fourth Amendment would amount to just words on paper and might as well be stricken from the Constitution.

Though Justice Stewart criticized Justice Clark for writing his opinion overruling *Wolf*, he ultimately came to the conclusion, as he told his audience in his lectures at Columbia Law School, that it was the right constitutional position.

Although the *Mapp* case made Dollree Mapp famous, it made state prosecutors throughout the land angry. The District Attorneys Association of the State of New York called on then-governor Nelson Rockefeller to join other states in asking the Supreme Court for reargument. The president of the association commented publicly that the *Mapp* decision would weaken law enforcement's fight against illegal drug trafficking. Echoing the cry of police chiefs and other prosecutors, he said, "If we are to serve in protecting our community, we must have adequate tools and practical procedures."[8] At the time, these complaints were unsuccessful. Even an effort by Congress to "overrule" the exclusionary rule in search and seizure cases failed to be implemented by federal prosecutors because they believed the statute passed to help them was unconstitutional. But, as we shall see, the angry protests against *Mapp* by state and federal law enforcement officials ultimately received a sympathetic hearing by the Supreme Court.

Coincidentally, as the rule articulated in her famous case began to be eroded by the post–Warren Supreme Court in the late 1960s, Dollree Mapp's fortunes also changed for the worse. Several years after her victory in the Supreme Court, Mapp moved to Queens County, New York. In 1970, her new home was raided by police, and this time they had a search warrant. They were Queens County narcotics detectives who later testified that they had kept Mapp under surveillance for six weeks as a suspected receiver of stolen property.[9] The searchers found and seized 50,000 envelopes containing heroin with a street value of $150,000 and stolen property valued at $100,000. The property included televisions, radios, fur pieces, typewriters, sets of silverware and pewterware, and an assortment of antiques, including clocks, vases, and candelabra.

Mapp was convicted at trial and sentenced under a stiff new state penalty law to twenty years to life.[10] Her arrest, trial, and conviction received special media coverage because of her famous Supreme Court case on which each news story covering her focused. In her state appeals as well as her appeal to the U.S. Court of Appeals for the Second Circuit, she challenged the legality of the search warrant used in the search of her home. Her lawyer claimed that the warrant was fraudulent and had been obtained by an officer who later was fired for corruption.

This time, Mapp was not successful in court. In 1981, however, she received a New Year's Eve commutation of her sentence by Governor Hugh Carey of New York, who acted in her case and in those of a number of other prisoners because they had been sentenced under the same stiff narcotics laws that Governor Carey later caused to be eased.[11] Dollree Mapp could now be paroled.

CHAPTER 8

Smothering the Flame

Suppressing unchallenged truth has set guilty criminals free but demonstrably has not deterred . . . violations of the Fourth Amendment . . . an anomalous and ineffective mechanism with which to regulate law enforcement.

Chief Justice Warren Burger, dissenting in
Bivens v. Six Unknown Federal Narcotics Agents, 403 U.S. 388
(1961)

The Bible says, "There arose a pharaoh who knew not Joseph." Supreme Court holdings interpreting Bill of Rights protections are similarly transient. Our popular belief that American constitutional principles of freedom are immutable—that objective and wise justices consistently declare the law of the land—is storied myth. In fact, the meaning of constitutional protections of the people is politically decided from time to time, depending on who is appointed to the Court. The Supreme Court's strong constitutional ruling in *Mapp* protecting the right of the people against illegal searches and seizures under the Fourth Amendment lasted only a little more than ten years.

Chief Justice Earl Warren resigned from the Supreme Court in 1969. He had presided during the 1960s over what has been called the Bill of Rights revolution—a reaffirmation and strengthening by the Court of the basic constitutional protections of the people, particularly those of persons accused in criminal cases. A new president was now in the White House—Richard Nixon. President Nixon, who showed his disdain for Fourth Amendment protections by his own violations, replaced Earl Warren as Chief Justice with a conservative Republican U.S. Court of Appeals judge, Warren E. Burger.

Warren Burger was born in 1907 in St. Paul, Minnesota. He was the fourth of seven children of Swiss and German parents. Too poor to attend college full time, Burger sold insurance while going to evening school at the University of Minnesota and St. Paul's College of Law (now Mitchell College of Law). He graduated from law school with honors in 1931 and practiced law in St. Paul. In 1953, he was appointed an assistant U.S. attorney general in the Lands Division of the U.S. Department of Justice. In 1956, President Eisenhower appointed him a judge of the U.S. Court of Appeals for the District of Columbia Circuit, where he served until his nomination to the Supreme Court.

In the opinions he wrote as a court of appeals judge, Burger demonstrated strong conservative positions. He was particularly pro–law enforcement in criminal cases and had a low opinion of the work of criminal defense lawyers. He was outspoken in his denunciation of the Fourth Amendment exclusionary rule, even though, as a court of appeals judge, he could have little influence in changing the rule after the Supreme Court's decision in Mapp. This changed, of course, when he became chief justice of the Supreme Court in 1969.

The earlier liberal majority of the Court—consisting of Warren, Douglas, Marshall, Brennan, Black, and Fortas, frequently joined by Stewart—was quickly eroded after Burger became chief justice. Justice Fortas retired in 1970 as a result of scandal. Justices Black and Harlan died in 1971. This gave President Nixon three new and controlling places on the Court to fill. Nixon chose two conservative Republicans and one conservative Democrat for these vacancies: Harry Blackmun, a Minnesota friend of Burger's; William Rehnquist, a high-ranking member of Nixon's Justice Department; and Lewis Powell (the Democrat), a corporation lawyer and former president of the American Bar Association.

Chief Justice Burger commanded a new conservative majority: Burger, White, Blackmun, Powell, and Rehnquist. In the beginning of his career on the Supreme Court, Blackmun voted with his friend Burger, so much so that they came to be called the "Minnesota twins." However, beginning with his controversial abortion rights opinion in *Roe v. Wade*, Blackmun became more independent and often voted with liberal members of the Court.

Burger's new majority was decidedly hostile to the Fourth Amendment exclusionary rule and seemingly to the Fourth Amendment itself. Consistent with President Nixon's law-and-order administration, these new justices set out to dismantle what they believed to be the overly broad protections of criminals created by the Warren Court. Particularly targeted was the exclusionary rule as defined by the Court in *Weeks* and *Mapp*.

Clearly, Chief Justice Burger and his supporters on the Court had the power to overrule these landmark cases. They either lacked the courage for such a frontal attack or did not want to send the wrong message to law enforcement officials that all restraints were off. Even before he gained his majority on the Court, Burger signaled his opposition to the exclusionary rule in his dissent in *Bivens v. Six Unknown Agents*[1] in 1971. He roundly assailed the suppression of unlawfully seized evidence as harmful to society and ineffective in restraining police violations of the Fourth Amendment because it did not "punish" the police, but only the prosecutor's case. To him, the exclusionary rule was merely a court-created rule of evidence announced by justices with good but completely mistaken intentions. It is interesting that Burger chose to take his stand against the exclusionary rule so early in his tenure and in this specific case.

Bivens was not an exclusion-of-evidence case. It came to the Court in the posture of a civil claim for damages against federal officers by an innocent person who had mistakenly become the victim of an unlawful search. The federal officers had unlawfully broken into Webster Bivens's apartment and seized and manacled him in front of his wife and children. They searched throughout the apartment, finding nothing, and threatened to arrest the entire family. The officers then took him to the federal courthouse where they strip-searched him and still found no evidence. Since no incriminating evidence had been found or seized, there was nothing to be excluded.

Bivens, acting as his own lawyer, claimed, nevertheless, that the violation of his Fourth Amendment rights required a remedy, such as money damages. The lower federal courts turned him down. The Supreme Court agreed to hear his case and ruled in Bivens's favor. In a majority opinion written by Justice Brennan, the Court held that the federal courts had the power to create a civil tort remedy of damages for a Fourth Amendment violation.

This case has been understood by lawyers and law professors alike as an exemplary decision providing an innocent victim of an illegal search and seizure with substantial financial redress against the violating federal officers. In fact, this understanding is wrong both as to the innocence of the victim and the substantialness of his financial recovery.

Far from being an innocent victim, Bivens was a petty drug peddler who wrote his petition to the Supreme Court from jail after having been convicted on narcotics charges in another case. The federal narcotics officers who had conducted the unlawful search had simply been unlucky on that occasion in finding no evidence. Also, after winning his case in the Supreme Court, Bivens realized a total of only five hundred dollars from the six offending narcotics officers in a settlement he willingly agreed to.

This case gives stark reality to the meaninglessness of money damages as a remedy for Fourth Amendment violations. In Bivens's case, he became convinced that, with his record, he would never get a substantial verdict from a jury. In addition, after his Supreme Court victory, federal officials so harassed him and threatened to put him in prison for many years that Bivens wisely concluded that it was better for him to be satisfied with the measly settlement.

Bivens's success in his own case in the Supreme Court made him a sought-after jailhouse lawyer. When he was released from prison, he formed an organization called Bivens Legal Assistance Movement (BLAM). BLAM offered legal assistance for prisoners claiming to have been the victims of illegal law enforcement conduct.

With the new Court appointments, Burger could now do more than declare his opposition to the exclusionary rule in dissent. But how was this new majority on the Court to tackle the exclusionary rule? Under the Court's prior holdings, the rule had become as integral a part of the Fourth Amendment as if it had been written into the Fourth Amendment. The language of Justice Day in *Weeks* and of Justice Clark in *Mapp* permitted no other interpretation. If Burger and his supporters read these opinions honestly, their only strategy would have to be to overrule them. For a number of reasons, they were not prepared to do this. Foremost among them was the concern Burger had expressed in his dissent in *Bivens* that overruling these precedents might give the wrong message to police that they could act without restraints. So Burger and his supporters chose to read *Weeks* and *Mapp* dishonestly. They accomplished this by (1) inventing a balancing test, (2) limiting the number of challenges to unlawful searches and seizures through the doctrine of "standing," and (3) creating a "good faith" exception. In this way, the new majority succeeded in enfeebling the Fourth Amendment itself and thereby eroding the protections against unreasonable searches and seizures.

The Balancing Test

Three cases decided by the Supreme Court in the 1970s gave the Burger majority its first opportunity to whittle away at *Weeks* and *Mapp* and the Fourth Amendment. In *United States v. Calandra* (1974),[2] *United States v. Janis* (1976),[3] and *Stone v. Powell* (1976),[4] evidence admittedly illegally seized by federal or state officials in violation of the Fourth Amendment was held by the new majority to be admissible, in each case overruling U.S. courts of appeals decisions that applied the exclusionary rule under the holdings of *Weeks* and *Mapp*. Each of these cases presented to the Court a different application of the exclusionary rule.

In *Calandra*, illegally seized records taken by federal agents from the offices of John Calandra, president of Royal Machine and Tool Company in Cleveland, Ohio, were used by a federal prosecutor as a basis to ask Mr. Calandra questions before a federal grand jury. Mr. Calandra refused to answer these questions first on the ground of his Fifth Amendment rights against self-incrimination and then, after being granted immunity, on the ground of his Fourth Amendment rights under the exclusionary rule.

The U.S. District Court supervising the grand jury ruled that the illegally seized records should be excluded from the grand jury and returned to Calandra and that no questions based on these records should be asked Calandra in the grand jury because they would be derived from the violation of his Fourth Amendment rights. The U.S. Court of Appeals for the Sixth Circuit affirmed the district court's rulings. These court rulings were completely consistent with the prior holdings of the Supreme Court in *Weeks* and *Mapp*, and that should have been the end of the case.

Indeed, in *Silverthorne Lumber Co. v. United States*,[5] a case interpreting *Weeks* in 1920, Justice Holmes declared that the exclusionary rule governing illegally acquired evidence by the government mandated "not merely [that] evidence so acquired shall not be used before the court but that it shall not be used at all." Nevertheless the Burger majority agreed to review *Calandra* on the government's petition, reversed the U.S. court of appeals, and held in an opinion written by Justice Powell that the exclusionary rule did not apply to the grand jury.

Janis presented a different exclusionary rule issue to the Court. Los Angeles police officers raided Max Janis's apartment and seized more than $4,000 in cash and a number of wagering records. The officers acted under a warrant that later was held to not be based on probable cause and, therefore, to be invalid. The evidence seized was suppressed by the Municipal Court of Los Angeles because it had been obtained in violation of Janis's Fourteenth Amendment rights. Shortly after the search of Janis's apartment, the officer in charge called an agent of the U.S. Internal Revenue Service and turned over the cash and records to the agent. On the basis of the wagering records, the IRS determined that Janis owed the federal government $89,026.09 in taxes and assessed him for that amount. Janis asked the IRS to return the cash illegally seized from him but was turned down. He then filed a civil suit against the IRS for his money. The IRS countersued for its assessment.

The U.S. district court ruled that Janis was entitled to the return of his money and that the IRS assessment against him should be quashed because it was based entirely on the records that had been illegally seized from Janis by the Los Angeles police. The U.S. Court of Appeals for the Ninth Circuit affirmed the district court's rulings. Once again, the decisions of these two federal courts were fully consistent with *Weeks*, *Mapp*, and *Silverthorne*, and the case should have stopped there. But the new majority agreed to review it on the government's petition and held, in an opinion written by Justice Blackmun, that the exclusionary rule was not applicable in a federal civil case where the evidence had been illegally seized by state officers.

Stone v. Powell represented yet another exclusionary rule issue: whether the Fourth Amendment exclusionary rule should be enforced by a federal court on a petition for a writ of habeas corpus filed by a state prisoner. The prisoner claimed that he had been imprisoned unconstitutionally because his state conviction was based on illegally seized evidence in violation of his Fourteenth Amendment rights, which the state courts had refused to exclude from evidence. The U.S. District Court for the Northern District of California refused to grant Powell's petition.

However, the U.S. Court of Appeals for the Ninth Circuit reversed the district court and held that federal court review on habeas corpus was always open to state prisoners claiming they were unconstitutionally confined. The court of appeals ruled that California's failure to exclude the illegally seized evidence in Powell's criminal case resulted in his being unconstitutionally confined in violation of his Fourteenth Amendment rights. Here, too, the court of appeals was following the precedents of the Supreme Court.

Still, in this case, also, the Burger majority, on the petition of the state of California, reversed the court of appeals and held, in an another opinion written by Justice Powell, that the exclusionary rule could not be raised by a state prisoner in a federal court on habeas corpus if that prisoner had been given a fair hearing by the state court on his Fourteenth Amendment claims. Incredibly, the new majority insisted on this denial of federal district court review on habeas corpus even if the state courts had been wrong in their Fourteenth Amendment rulings, that is, even if the state prisoner was unconstitutionally confined by the state.

In these three cases, the Burger majority downgraded the exclusionary rule to merely a court-created prophylactic remedy. How did they get around the strong constitutional rulings of *Weeks* and *Mapp*? In essence, they ignored these cases and made up their own precedent, taking a "long step toward abandonment of the exclusionary rule," as Justice Brennan charged in his dissent in *Calandra*. The majority evaded the clear rulings of these prior cases that the exclusionary rule was a constitutionally mandated right inherent in the Fourth Amendment because it was an essential part of that amendment, as Justices Brennan and Marshall argued in their dissents in *Calandra* and *Janis*. Instead, the new majority introduced the concept that the exclusionary rule was a convenient creation of the Court to be applied at the discretion of the Court whenever the Court believed it served what the majority now concluded to be its sole purpose—deterrence.

Underlying this concept was another new principle formulated by the majority that Fourth Amendment protections of the individual are not always guaranteed but must be always balanced against the costs to society of enforcing these protections. According to this new balancing test, the Court claimed the discretion not to enforce its own created remedy to protect Fourth Amendment rights if, in enforcing them, societal costs would be too high. This balancing rule is not only not reflected in any way in *Weeks* or *Mapp* or in any of the prior cases interpreting them, it runs contrary to the philosophy of the framers of the Bill of Rights. If anything, the Bill of Rights was meant to protect the individual against government representing societal majorities. If an individual may only have such protections when the Court believes society will not be threatened by them, of what value are they? The uniqueness of individual freedom as guaranteed by the Constitution and its amendments making up the Bill of Rights is that the individual can safely stand against the will of society within the coverage of these protections.

Having stripped the exclusionary rule of its constitutional underpinnings by making it a court-created discretionary remedy, the new majority proceeded to define how the Court should exercise its discretion. They reduced the purpose of the rule to the single one of deterrence of future police misconduct. They rejected any consideration of the rule as a constitutional right of the individual or as essential to preserve judicial integrity by not having courts condone police illegality by letting police benefit from the fruits of their unlawful conduct. Both of these purposes of the rule were fundamental foundations of the *Weeks* and *Mapp* rulings.

Thus, if the only purpose of the rule is to deter future police misconduct, the majority concluded, it should only be applied when the Court is convinced that excluding the evidence in a specific case would significantly deter future police misconduct. But by what criteria would the Court make that determination? Chief Justice Burger in his dissent in *Bivens* had insisted that there was no empirical evidence that the exclusionary rule was a significant deterrent to police violations of the Fourth Amendment. He said that the police were too busy fighting crime to read Supreme Court decisions. Of course, there also was no empirical evidence that the rule did not serve as a significant deterrence.

An honest reading of *Mapp* can lead only to the conclusions that, first, the exclusionary rule serves much higher purposes than merely deterrence, and second, it is a necessary and essential remedy to permit the Fourth Amendment to work, to be more than a pious statement on paper. With this as its premise, the Court in *Mapp* actually found that the exclusionary rule was implied in the Fourth Amendment, which meant that its need did not have to be further litigated in each case. Once and for all, the exclusionary rule was necessary to provide the people the protection the Fourth Amendment guaranteed them.

The new majority now turned this holding of the Court in *Mapp* on its head. Despite having recognized that the exclusionary rule was meant to give effectiveness to the Fourth Amendment, they held in *Calandra*, *Janis*, and *Stone* that the Court would decide on a case-by-case basis when the Fourth Amendment needed to be helped by the exclusionary rule. Their application of the new discretionary test in these three cases proved, at the least, that it was untenable and, at the most, that it was dishonest.

For example, Justice Powell's deployment of his discretionary balancing and deterrence test in *Calandra* displays incredible ignorance of the operations of the criminal justice system, or, less kind, a willingness to blind himself to what he must have known. Using deterrence of future police misconduct as his criterion for enforcing the exclusionary rule, Justice Powell concluded that police officers will not be significantly deterred from Fourth Amendment violations if illegally seized evidence is excluded in grand jury proceedings. Police officers, he claimed, don't even think about the grand jury when they contemplate searches. He was satisfied that the deterrent function of the rule is accomplished if such evidence is excluded at trial.

Any experienced prosecutor or police officer could tell Justice Powell that only a minority of criminal cases go to trial; that in most cases, after indictment, there is a plea bargain leading to a conviction of the defendant without any review of Fourth Amendment violations. So much for the exclusion of illegally seized evidence at trial as a deterrent! On the other hand, successful plea bargaining could not take place without a grand jury indictment, which serves as the formal charge against the defendant, authorizing trial. For this reason, it is to the advantage of the prosecutor and the police to obtain a grand jury indictment, even on the basis of illegally obtained evidence. Prosecutors and police officers know this and make it part of their strategy of law enforcement.

Thus, if illegally seized evidence were excluded in the grand jury proceedings, prosecutors would be less likely to obtain indictments, plea bargains, and convictions. Consequently, the majority should have realized that a contrary ruling, consistent with *Weeks* and *Mapp*, would have resulted in pressure from prosecutors on police officers, including providing more police training, to ensure that the police conducted lawful searches and seizures. Far from serving the new majority's own deterrence theory, their ruling in *Calandra* serves, instead, to encourage Fourth Amendment violations by police to get the evidence needed to obtain an indictment and a plea bargain, which will assure no court review of their unlawful conduct. In his dissent in *Janis*, Justice Stewart strongly made a similar point:

> The Court's failure to heed these precedents (*Weeks, Mapp,* and *Silverthorne*) not only rips a hole in the fabric of the law but leads to a result that cannot even serve the valid arguments of those who would eliminate the exclusionary rule entirely. For under the Court's ruling society must not only continue to pay the high cost of the exclusionary rule (by forgoing criminal convictions which can be obtained only on the basis of illegally seized evidence) but it must also forfeit the benefit for which it has paid so dearly.

Justice Blackmun's reasoning in *Janis* supporting the admissibility of state officers' illegally seized evidence in a federal civil tax case is equally flawed. Justice Blackmun could not have been so naive as to be unaware of the strong linkage between a state's enforcement of its criminal gambling laws and federal tax enforcement agents. It is public knowledge that organized crime bosses who ran the highly profitable illegal gambling operations, like Al Capone and Mickey Cohen, were less concerned about local court punishments, usually small fines, than they were about federal tax and racketeering convictions with their substantial prison sentences. Indeed, Capone and Cohen were convicted in federal court and sent to federal prisons after state and federal law enforcement cooperated in arresting and prosecuting them.

In *Janis* itself, the state arresting officer immediately contacted a federal IRS agent and got him involved in a tax case against Janis. The local police know that they can hit local gamblers hard only by leveraging their cases into federal tax cases. Justice Stewart, in his dissent in *Janis*, ridiculed the majority's lack of insight and candor on the real world of state and federal law enforcement cooperation in such cases and on the flaws in their deterrence reasoning. After discussing the common knowledge about federal and state law enforcement cooperation in enforcing criminal wagering laws, Stewart stated: "If state police officials can effectively crack down on gambling law violators by the simple expedient of violating their constitutional rights and turning the illegally seized evidence over to Internal Revenue Service agents on the proverbial 'silver platter,' then the deterrent purpose of the exclusionary rule is wholly frustrated." Quoting from *Elkins v. United States*, Justice Stewart added, "If, on the other hand, it is understood that the fruits of an unlawful search by state agents will be inadmissible in a federal trial, there can be no inducement to subterfuge and evasion with respect to federal-state cooperation in criminal investigation."

Finally, in *Stone v. Powell*, the new majority continued in its business, as Justice Brennan complained in *Janis*, of "slow strangulation" of the exclusionary rule. Once again, Justice Powell engaged in an assumption about the deterrent impact of the exclusionary rule he had to know was false. This time, he claimed that state police would not be significantly deterred from violating the Fourth Amendment if a federal court freed a state prisoner on habeas corpus on the ground he had been unconstitutionally convicted by the state court's admission of illegally seized evidence.

Without any factual record to support him, Justice Powell declared that a state police officer has no concern about a federal habeas corpus action when he conducts searches and seizures and would therefore not be influenced by a federal habeas corpus decision holding that a search and seizure he made was illegal. The history of federal habeas corpus review of state convictions reveals this view to be nonsense. Many of the Supreme Court's constitutional decisions limiting state law enforcement conduct had come up to the Court through habeas corpus petitions filed in federal courts by state prisoners. These included cases involving state violations of the Fourth Amendment.

Not only did local police know about federal court reversals of their convictions through habeas corpus, they angrily protested what they believed to be overreaching by the federal courts into their business. State prosecutors and state courts also resented the federal intervention.[6] Federal habeas corpus review of state convictions was on the agenda of meetings by the International Association of Chiefs of Police, the

National District Attorneys Association, and state court conferences. Clearly, local police, who had become comfortable with their state court's winking at their Fourth Amendment violations, worried about the backlash on their work that could be caused by federal court reversals on habeas corpus.

Besides, the deterrence issue was a red herring in *Stone v. Powell.* That question was not a relevant part of the state court decisions and should not have been relevant on the petition for a writ of habeas corpus. The new majority did not disagree that the state prisoner in this case had been unconstitutionally convicted and was confined by the state in violation of his Fourteenth Amendment rights. The U.S. Court of Appeals for the Ninth Circuit had so held, and Justice Powell in his opinion did not challenge that holding. He held only that, despite whether the state prisoner was unconstitutionally confined, he was not entitled to raise the issue of the exclusionary rule on a petition for a writ of habeas corpus.

This holding is baseless for two reasons. The federal statute (28 U.S.C. §2254) under which the state prisoner in *Stone v. Powell* filed his habeas corpus petition mandates that a state prisoner should be granted the petition by the federal court if he establishes he was in custody in violation of the Constitution. That is the only issue before the Court on habeas corpus. Justice Powell's limiting the right to habeas corpus on the basis of his deterrence theory directly violated the act of Congress without a valid constitutional theory.

The second reason the holding is baseless is that, as Justice Brennan argued in his dissent, it makes no sense. Justice Powell's holding only applied to a habeas corpus petition. However, if this same state prisoner had filed a petition for a writ of certiorari to the Supreme Court for review of his state conviction on the same Fourteenth Amendment constitutional ground, the unconstitutionality of his custody would not have been questioned, and the Court would have jurisdiction to reverse the state conviction. Yet Justice Powell holds that the same prisoner is not in custody in violation of the Constitution on Fourteenth Amendment grounds when this issue is raised in a federal habeas corpus petition. Justice Brennan exclaimed in his dissent, "In short, it escapes me as to what logic can support the assertion that the defendant's unconstitutional confinement obtains during the process of direct review, no matter how long that process takes, but the unconstitutionality then suddenly dissipates at the moment the claim is asserted on habeas corpus."

The clue, perhaps, to the illogic of Justice Powell's reasoning is that Powell and his supporters on the Court chose in this case to redefine the right of habeas corpus in a way contrary to the ancient tradition of that right, to the Court's prior decisions, and to the clear meaning of congressional legislation. The new majority now limits the right to habeas corpus only to those state prisoners who can show that the constitutional violation in their case affected the truth-finding function of the criminal judicial process. Only those who can show that they may be innocent need apply.

Thus, according to Justice Powell, although a defendant is convicted or imprisoned on the basis of evidence seized in violation of the Fourth or Fourteenth Amendments of the U.S. Constitution, he is still guilty of the crime and, therefore, is not deserving of federal habeas relief. This arbitrary new restriction on habeas corpus and the Bill of Rights is unsupported by any of the many precedents of the Supreme Court on habeas corpus.

Justice Brennan, in his dissent, refers to and quotes from many of these prior holdings. What they all have held again and again is that "habeas jurisdiction is a deterrent to unconstitutional actions [of any kind] by trial and appellate judges, and a safeguard to ensure that rights secured under the constitution and federal laws are not merely honored in the breach. . . . The historical function of the writ of habeas corpus is that of an effective and imperative remedy for detentions contrary to fundamental law."

Justice Clark's opinion in *Mapp*, which Justice Powell does not overrule, illustrates the poverty of the new majority's position and the danger of its threat to individual freedom. Justice Clark reminded us that in a truly free society, it is not enough to convict the guilty—they must be convicted under the rule of law. We cannot tolerate even the conviction of a guilty person in violation of the Constitution and rule of law. Unlike Justice Powell, Justice Clark accepted the fact that enforcement of the Fourth Amendment exclusionary rule might free a guilty person. But, as he said, "It is the law that frees him."

Who May Assert the Fourth Amendment Protection: Standing

Having ruled that the courts have discretion to decide when the right of the people under the Fourth Amendment will be protected, the new majority of the Supreme Court proceeded to dilute that protection even further by drastically limiting who among the people may be given that protection. The court chose an obscure robbery case from Illinois to make this additional incursion in Fourth Amendment rights.

A police officer on routine motor patrol received a radio call of a robbery of a clothing store in Bourbonnais, Illinois, that described the getaway car. The officer then spotted an automobile "which he thought might be the getaway car." He radioed for assistance, and he and several other officers stopped the car. The occupants were ordered out of the car, and two officers searched the vehicle, finding a box of rifle shells in the locked glove compartment and a sawed-off rifle under the front passenger seat. Only the passengers, and not the owner who was the driver, were charged with robbery.

Under the law at that time, the stopping of the car and the search and seizure of its contents were unlawful, in violation of the Fourteenth Amendment, because the officer's speculation that the car was involved in the robbery could not meet either the requirement of probable cause, which was essential for a valid arrest or search, or the standard of reasonable suspicion necessary for a stop and frisk. Also, under the Supreme Court decision of *Jones v. United States*,[7] each of the passengers would have standing to raise the search and seizure issue and move to suppress the seized evidence. Justice Frankfurter, in that ruling, held that anyone legitimately on the premises where an unlawful search occurred had their reasonable expectation of privacy violated under the Constitution and were entitled to the protections of the Fourth and Fourteenth Amendments.

However, the new majority, through Chief Justice Rehnquist, ruled otherwise in the Illinois robbery case, *Rakas v. Illinois*.[8] They held that mere passengers in an automobile, though legitimately there, had too casual a relationship to the proprietorship of the car to be entitled to a legitimate expectation of privacy while in the car and, therefore, had no standing to challenge the search and seizure. Chief Justice Rehnquist also said that since none of the passengers claimed ownership of the shells or rifle, they had no standing to move to suppress them as evidence, even if they were seized in violation of the Constitution.

Apparently basing the constitutional protection against unreasonable searches and seizures on property rights, the ruling of the majority flew in the face of Justice Frankfurter's opinion in *Jones*. There, Frankfurter decried earlier rulings, which favored property interests in enforcing the Fourth Amendment. He stated clearly that the Fourth Amendment does not protect "arcane property interests," but protects the right of privacy. It was in this context that Frankfurter upheld the right of Jones, who was a guest in an apartment, and not the owner or tenant, to challenge an unlawful search and seizure in the apartment. He ruled that Jones's legitimate presence in the apartment gave him a reasonable expectation of privacy there.

Similarly, the Supreme Court, in *Katz v. United States*,[9] held that the user of a telephone booth, not the owner but legitimately there to use the telephone, had a reasonable expectation of privacy in the booth and had the right to challenge a government's unlawful recording of his conversation. In his opinion written for the Court, Justice Stewart also emphasized that the government's unlawful conduct did not have to be an intrusion in a proprietary space of the target, but only in a place where the person complaining had a reasonable expectation of privacy.

When confronted with these decisions by the dissenters in *Rakas*, Chief Justice Rehnquist disclaimed any intention to rely on property interests for enforcement of the Fourth Amendment. However, his own words belied this disclaimer. In distinguishing *Jones*, which he did not overrule, he said that Jones had a reasonable expectation of privacy in the apartment as a guest because he had a key to the apartment and could exclude others. Nowhere in Frankfurter's opinion in *Jones* was this property distinction used. Also, Chief Justice Rehnquist claimed *Katz* was decided differently because the defendant there paid for the right to be in the booth by placing the requisite coin in the telephone box. Again, Justice Stewart never relied on this property interest in finding that Katz had a reasonable expectation of privacy in the booth.

By arbitrarily mandating this restriction on who may challenge an unlawful search and seizure on the basis of property interests, the new majority has destroyed much of the deterrence value of the exclusionary rule. Under this ruling, law enforcement officers can confidently ignore constitutional protections in many more instances, secure in the knowledge that even if their conduct is unlawful, the victim will be unable to raise this issue. This makes little sense even within the expressed philosophy of the new majority, which has limited the application of the exclusionary rule to deterrence of future police misconduct. It clearly is not enough for the Court to say, as Justice Rehnquist did in *Rakas*, that sufficient deterrence will be provided by those who do have standing to raise Fourth Amendment issues. Suffice it to say that prosecutors and police will avoid these challenges by arresting and charging only the passengers in cars, as they did in *Rakas*.

Justice White, who usually voted with the new majority, wrote a strong dissent, which was joined in by Justices Brennan, Marshall, and Stevens. White found the *Jones* standard (legitimately on the premises) much more consistent with the language and purposes of the Fourth Amendment. He complained that the majority's holding was "contrary not only to our past decisions and the logic of the Fourth Amendment, but also to the everyday expectations of privacy that we share."

More important, White accused the majority that in "its rush to limit the applicability of the exclusionary rule somewhere, anywhere, the court ignored procedure, logic, and common sense to exclude the rule's operation from situations in which, paradoxically, it is justified and needed." White claimed the majority mutilated its own earlier emphasis for deterrence in applying the exclusionary rule. He said:

> More importantly, the ruling today undercuts the force of the exclusionary rule in the one area in which its use is most certainly justified—the deterrence of bad-faith violations of the Fourth Amendment. . . . This decision invites police to engage in patently unreasonable searches every time an automobile contains more than one occupant. . . . After this decision, police will have little to lose by unreasonably searching a vehicle occupied by more than one person.

Thus, by redefining the circumstances under which a person is permitted to have a reasonable expectation of privacy, the Court has not only limited the exclusionary rule, it has narrowed the application of the Fourth Amendment itself. The new majority proceeded to apply this very strategy in broader areas than car searches. For example, it held that a person who is invited as a guest to a friend's home has no reasonable expectation of privacy in that home. Even if police break in unlawfully, search the home, and seize evidence implicating the guest, the Court ruled that the guest's Fourth Amendment rights are not violated and the evidence can be used against him.[10]

The only exception the Court has made to this denial of Fourth Amendment protection has been in the case of a guest who is invited to stay overnight. Deferring to what it found to be the American tradition and culture of guests staying overnight at a friend's house, the Court was willing to bestow on such guests a reasonable expectation of privacy.[11]

However, even the homeowner may lose the reasonable privacy rights he normally has in his own home under the Fourth Amendment. If the police, using a helicopter, hover in navigable space above the house and photograph growing marijuana through a skylight in the roof or a hothouse in the yard, they have not, according to the new majority, violated the Fourth Amendment rights of the homeowner.[12] These justices reason that the homeowner has no reasonable expectation of privacy from police observation of anything in his house or yard while they are above the house in navigable air space. This ruling holds even if the homeowner has put up a high fence around his house to both announce and preserve his privacy.

On similar reasoning, the Court has even gone further in denying Fourth Amendment protections of a citizen from police searches of what most people would believe would reflect their most intimate and private activities. Despite the titillation many newspaper readers felt about stories that reporters for the *National Enquirer* had rummaged through the trash cans behind Secretary of State Henry Kissinger's house, most people in America do not expect the police to be going through their trash cans. Nevertheless, the Laguna Beach, California, police did search the contents of sealed garbage bags Billy Greenwood had put in his lidded trash can, and they found traces of cocaine. On this evidence, they obtained a search warrant to search Greenwood's house. There they found more evidence of cocaine trafficking and arrested Greenwood.

The California Supreme Court held that police search of a person's closed trash can, put out on the sidewalk awaiting the trash collector, violated the Fourteenth Amendment and made the seizure of the evidence of cocaine in the trash can and later in the house unlawful. On California's petition, the Supreme Court agreed to review the case. In the majority opinion, written by Justice Byron White, the Court reversed the California court ruling. Justice White wrote that once a person puts his trash out to be collected by the trash collector, he has no further reasonable expectation of privacy in the trash. White pointed out that vandals, children, or animals could spill out the trash from the can, and we would not expect the police to avert their eyes from what they can see on the sidewalk.

Do people really not continue to expect privacy concerning the intimate things they include in their trash while the trash is still collected together in a can that identifies them? Was Justice White speaking of the real-life experiences of people? In a strong dissent, Justice William Brennan challenged White's conclusions as incompatible with the privacy expectations of most Americans. He wrote that the majority had ignored considering what private things people throw out in their trash, not expecting anyone to examine them. To illustrate how a person's entire lifestyle and intimate and private activities can be "read" in that person's trash, Brennan wrote, "Scrutiny of another's trash is contrary to commonly accepted notions of civilized behavior. I suspect, therefore, that members of our society will be shocked to learn that the Court, the ultimate guarantor of liberty, deems unreasonable our expectation that the aspects of our private lives that are concealed safely in a trash bag will not become public." Then Brennan vividly described what aspects of our private lives can be found in trash bags:

> Almost every human activity ultimately manifests itself in waste products. . . . A single bag of trash testifies elegantly to the eating, reading, and recreational habits of the person who produced it. A search of trash, like a search of the bedroom, can relate intimate details about sexual practices, health, and personal hygiene. Like rifling through desk drawers or intercepting phone calls, rummaging through trash can divulge the

target's financial and professional status, political affiliations and inclinations, private thoughts, personal relationships, and romantic interests. It cannot be doubted that a sealed trash can harbors telling evidence of the intimate activity associated with the sanctity of a man's home and the privacies of life, which the Fourth Amendment is designed to protect. (Quotation marks and citations omitted.)

In the midst of this narrowing of Fourth Amendment protections, the new majority—through one of its most aggressive members, Justice Anthony Scalia—unexpectedly sided with a homeowner's Fourth Amendment rights. It was a unique case, involving scientific collection of evidence. In *Kyllo v. United States*,[13] an agent of the United States Department of the Interior, suspecting that marijuana was being grown by a man named Kyllo inside his home, decided to use a thermal imaging device to scan the building. This device could help the agent determine whether the amount of heat emanating from the home was consistent with the use of the high-intensity lamps typically required for growing marijuana indoors. The scan, which took only a few minutes, was performed at 3:20 a.m. from the passenger seat of the agent's vehicle across the street from the front of, and also from the street in the back of, the home. The scan found parts of the home hotter than other parts and considerably warmer than other homes in the neighborhood.

The agent concluded from the scan that the homeowner was using halide lights to grow marijuana in the home. With this evidence, information from informers, and the utility bills for the home, federal agents obtained a search warrant from a federal magistrate and in the course of the search found an indoor growing operation involving one hundred marijuana plants. Kyllo's motion to suppress the marijuana, based on the argument that it had been seized as a result of an unlawful intrusion into the privacy of his home through the use of the thermal imaging device, was denied by the U.S. district court. The court ruled that the scan by the device did not intrude into the home but measured heat emanating out of the home, in public, where the agent had a right to be. The U.S. court of appeals affirmed the ruling of the district court.

The Supreme Court agreed to review the case and, in an opinion by Justice Scalia, reversed the conviction. Justice Scalia wrote that government use of such advanced scientific methods of collecting evidence from inside a home violated the homeowner's Fourth Amendment rights. He disagreed with the lower courts that the thermal imaging device only measured heat that was in the public space outside the home. Justice Scalia was troubled that such a scan captured activity going on inside the home and cautioned that scientific advancements in this technology would give police capability to see inside the home, even inside a person's bathroom.

The *Kyllo* case suggests that even justices who support restricting Fourth Amendment protections in ordinary criminal cases are not ready to allow the government, without judicial supervision, to engage in what can be considered the functional equivalent of invasion of private homes through the use of ever advancing scientific technology. In part, Justice Scalia's cautious approach in *Kyllo* may represent the same uncertainty and trepidation most of us feel about where the advancing technology will lead us.

This view of the conservative members of the Court is significant in light of the domestic "war on terrorism." Federal agencies, under pressure to proactively intercept suspected terrorist activity, are supporting research and development projects to advance technology far beyond its existing capability to a status that will permit federal investigators to collect and integrate complete data on the personal, political, religious, social, financial, and all other aspects of the lives of citizens and noncitizens in the United States. The government hopes such advances in technology will help it develop more accurate profiles of potential terrorists. *Kyllo* is a warning signal from the Court that the government's success in attaining greater technological ability to identify terrorist activity may involve additional invasions of individual privacy sufficient to cross the border of Fourth Amendment protections.

The Good Faith Exception

The new majority extended its balancing test to refuse to exclude unlawfully seized evidence at the criminal trial even if the evidence was seized in violation of the accused's own constitutional rights. In *United States v. Leon*,[14] local Burbank, California, police had raided Alberto Leon's house in Glendale, California, on the basis of a magistrate-issued search warrant that was invalid because it was not supported by probable cause. A quantity of marijuana was seized during this search and turned over to federal authorities. Leon was indicted and prosecuted in the U.S. District Court for the Central District of California. The district court judge suppressed the marijuana evidence on the ground that it was seized under an invalid warrant in violation of the Fourth Amendment. The U.S. Court of Appeals for the Ninth Circuit affirmed the ruling of the district court.

The Justice Department sought review by the U.S. Supreme Court on a petition that conceded the search had been unlawful but asked the Court to not enforce the exclusionary rule where an officer has acted in reasonably good faith reliance on a warrant issued by a magistrate even though the warrant, itself, is invalid. The Court agreed to review the case and reversed the decision by the Ninth Circuit in an opinion by Justice White following the government's recommendation of a good faith exception to the exclusionary rule.

How does the good faith of the officer erase a clear violation of the Fourth Amendment? The Court had refused to consider such an argument in past cases. Now, however, with the invention of the balancing test, the new majority was ready to turn wrong into right. Starting again with the Court's recently revised purpose of the exclusionary rule—that it was created by the Court solely for deterring future police misconduct—Justice White concluded that excluding the evidence in *Leon*, where the officers acted in good faith reliance on the warrant issued by the magistrate even though the Fourth Amendment had been violated, would not serve to significantly deter future police misconduct. White reasoned that if the officer did not believe, at the time, that he was doing anything wrong, how would later exclusion of the evidence deter him from engaging again in what he still thought was legal but was, in fact, an unlawful search and seizure?

Of course, the specific language of the Fourth Amendment protects the right of the people against *all* unreasonable searches and seizures. There is no qualification in the application of this Bill of Rights protection where unreasonable searches and seizures are conducted by the government mistakenly or in good faith ignorance that they are unlawful. The violation of this fundamental right occurs whether the government acts maliciously or with good intention.

By recognizing this good faith exception, Justice White and the new majority took the mistakenly narrow position that the remedy of the exclusionary rule was meant to be punitive—a punishment of the erring police officer. Aside from the fact that police officers are, indeed, not punished by the exclusion of evidence obtained illegally but are usually rewarded for these searches and arrests, the true deterrent value of the exclusionary rule is its educational impact on police conduct. Justice Brennan, in his dissent, assailed the majority's wrongheaded view of the exclusionary rule as a punishment of the police officer and emphasized that even in the case of an officer acting in good faith, the exclusionary rule served an important educational function. He declared:

> If the overall educational effect of the exclusionary rule is considered, application of the rule to even those situations in which individual police officers acted on the basis of a reasonable but mistaken belief that their conduct was authorized can still be expected to have a considerable long-term deterrent effect. If evidence is consistently excluded in these circumstances, police departments will surely be prompted to devote

> greater care and attention to providing sufficient information
> to establish probable cause when applying for a warrant . . .
> rather than automatically assuming that whatever document
> the magistrate has signed will necessarily comport with Fourth
> Amendment requirements.

However, even assuming that Justice White was right about the police officer who acts in good faith reliance on a warrant issued by a magistrate, what about the magistrate him- or herself? Is not the magistrate also bound by the requirements of the Fourth Amendment, and would not exclusion of the evidence where the magistrate has issued an unlawful warrant serve to deter future misconduct or mistakes by the magistrate? Remember, Justice Day, in his ruling that the exclusionary rule was an essential part of the Fourth Amendment in *Weeks v. United States*, stated that judges were just as much obligated to comply with the Fourth Amendment as law enforcement officers. He added that it was a judicial imperative to exclude evidence that had been seized unconstitutionally.

Amazingly, White ruled that the exclusionary rule was not intended to be applied to magistrates, only to police officers. He concluded gratuitously that the magistrate does not have a stake in the criminal case and, therefore, would not be deterred by exclusion of the evidence. This absurd position totally ignores the integration of the U.S. criminal justice system and the binding application of the Constitution to every part of the system.

If not magistrates, what about prosecutors? If they lose cases because of unlawful searches, even those conducted by officers in good faith, is it not likely that they will insist on better training of the police in Fourth Amendment requirements? Justice White ignores this issue. The new majority followed up its blind approach to the realities of the criminal justice system when it later held that evidence will not be excluded when it is seized by a police officer under the authority of a state statute that is held to be unconstitutional by the Court in violation of the Fourth Amendment.[15] The new majority also completely ignored the question of whether excluding the evidence would deter the legislators from enacting future unconstitutional statutes if the evidence was excluded! The Court must have assumed that state legislatures, too, have no stake in criminal cases.

The agenda of the new majority in destroying the remedy of the exclusionary rule without overruling *Weeks* and *Mapp* was clearly signaled by Justice Brennan in his dissent in *Leon*. He pronounced the following epitaph to the exclusionary rule:

> Ten years ago in *United States v. Calandra*...I expressed the fear that the Court's decision "may signal that a majority of my colleagues have positioned themselves to reopen the door [to evidence secured by official lawlessness] still further and abandon altogether the exclusionary rule in search and seizure cases." . . . Since then, in case after case, I have witnessed the Court's gradual but determined strangulation of the rule. It now appears that the Court's victory over the Fourth Amendment is complete. That today's decision represents the *pièce de résistance* of the Court's past efforts cannot be doubted, for today, the Court sanctions the use in the prosecution's case-in-chief of illegally obtained evidence against an individual whose rights have been violated—a result that had previously been thought to be foreclosed.

By the end of the twentieth century, federal and state law enforcement officials, with the aid of the conservative majority of the Supreme Court, enjoyed, for the most part, all the authority they could wish for to search persons and places and to seize almost anything related to suspected criminal conduct. The right of the people to be protected against unreasonable searches and seizures declared in the Fourth Amendment to the Constitution was once again mere words on paper. The Court had largely abandoned the enforcement strategies of its earlier rulings in *Weeks* and *Mapp* to make the Fourth Amendment protection effective.

Thus, law enforcement power had never been greater in the United States than at the beginning of the new millennium. This was particularly so on September 11, 2001.

CHAPTER 9

War on Terror: Security and Liberty

They that would give up essential liberty to obtain a little temporary safety deserve neither liberty nor safety.

Benjamin Franklin, 1759

When the hijacked airliners crashed into the twin towers of the World Trade Center in New York, into the Pentagon in Virginia just outside Washington, and into a field in Pennsylvania on the bright sunny morning of September 11, 2001, America changed from a land at peace on its own soil to a land under attack by international terrorists. Thousands of innocent people—men, women, and children—had been ruthlessly murdered. Not only Americans were killed; the carnage included citizens from many nations who were in the World Trade Center at the time. This was clearly a horrible American and world tragedy.

As in prior times of danger threatening our nation, our democratic government had to plan for security against future attack. Once again, we confronted the question of whether a free society, under a Constitution that defines the people as sovereign, and under a Bill of Rights that protects the personal freedoms of the citizenry from abuse by government, can be made adequately secure from such attacks without surrendering its freedom. In short, just how durable and strong are U.S. constitutional principles of freedom and individual liberty? Is it true, as U.S. government officials in times of crisis often claim, that such principles are workable only in periods of calm and peace, and cannot be afforded in times of crisis and emergency?

The revolutionary generation that founded this country answered this question clearly and defiantly by their rhetoric and commitment. They declared that this nation's strength and security were entirely based on and dependent on the liberty of the people under their new Constitution. If this liberty had to be surrendered under attack, they believed they might just as well have remained colonists under England's control. The courage they displayed fighting England for independence and freedom is the courage that has made America strong, free, and able to protect itself from its enemies.

President George W. Bush dramatically expressed this same stand when he rallied our nation to come together and strike back against those who attacked us. He declared that the terrorists struck us on September 11 to destroy our freedom, and he pledged for all Americans that the terrorists would utterly fail in this goal. Unfortunately, in the near panic that followed, Mr. Bush's government, particularly his attorney general, John Ashcroft, retreated to a formula for security that emphasized the need for the people to sacrifice freedom in the face of the dangers that threatened them. He pushed through Congress emergency legislation that weakened Fourth Amendment protections of the people even further than the Supreme Court has been willing to go.

Moreover, the government wrapped its declared need for restrictions on liberty in the cloak of American patriotism, sending the message that disagreement with such policies amounted to betrayal of American loyalty and giving aid to the terrorists. This threat succeeded in chilling debate, even in Congress, where the surge for bipartisanship smothered the evaluation and challenge that is essential in a democracy.

With the blessings of the United Nations, the United States sent its military forces to strike at the Taliban government in Afghanistan and at the al Qaeda terrorists, led by Osama Bin Laden, that the Taliban government supported and who had planned and carried out the 9/11 attacks in the United States. The Bush administration used the wartime conditions that followed to call for even tighter restrictions on individual liberty. Government leaders constantly cautioned American citizens that the war on terrorism would last a long time and emergency restrictions would continue to be necessary. To better organize against future terrorists' attacks inside the United States, the president pushed through an acquiescent Congress a new department of government, the Department of Homeland Security, in which a number of existing departments and agencies were merged.

Moreover, America's preemptive war on Iraq, which destroyed the Saddam Hussein regime, and subsequent government warnings of additional terrorist attacks on Americans and their allies have put the nation on a near-permanent emergency status. At least, as the president has announced, wartime restrictions will be necessary for a very long time. This has changed the very nature of our free society. Whatever resilience our constitutional freedoms have to enable them to endure during temporary serious incursions on individual liberties, such an indefinite period of repressive measures surely must threaten irreversible harm to the liberty rights of Americans.

The Bush administration's efforts to restrict liberty in response to threats to the United States are not unique in the history of our country. Unfortunately, that history has not been a proud one with regard to our government's commitment to liberty in such times of crisis. Every time that the country has acceded to the demands such as those the Bush administration is now making, it has lived to regret it.

During the administration of the second president of the United States, John Adams, war with France under its unstable revolutionary government loomed. French warships were attacking U.S. commercial ships in the Atlantic Ocean and the Caribbean Sea. Adams asked the Federalist-led Congress to provide for a stronger navy to combat the French ships, and he sent emissaries to France to demand that the French government show respect for the new nation of the United States. Thomas Jefferson's Republican Party opposed the Federalists' hostility to

France. A number of French aliens, hosted by Republicans, had come to America, and the Federalists suspected them of plotting against the United States. Republican newspaper editors viciously attacked President Adams and the Federalist leadership in Congress, accusing the Federalists of plotting to make the country a monarchy and Adams of seeking to become the monarch.

Outraged, the Federalists pushed through Congress the Alien and Sedition Acts, which authorized the government to seize and deport the French aliens and to arrest and criminally prosecute the Republican newspaper editors and other critics who daily denounced the Federalist government. An aggressive enforcer of the Sedition Act was Samuel Chase, a justice of the Supreme Court, who sentenced a number of newspaper editors to long prison terms after presiding as judge at trials in which he dominated the jury.

This was a dark period for liberty in the United States. Adams, who later tried to disassociate himself from the legislation, was tarnished by it. Adams and the Federalist leaders were not alone to blame. George Washington, in his retirement at Mount Vernon, enthusiastically and publicly supported the Alien and Sedition Acts. Formerly venerated as a beloved symbol of the new democracy, Washington himself had not been spared from the Republican attacks. The country came to regret this oppressive legislation, which was later allowed to expire, as an abusive overreaction by the government, inconsistent with American principles of freedom.

Only fifty years later, however, President Abraham Lincoln, in the midst of the Civil War, reemployed sedition laws to imprison critics of his handling of the war. He also, by executive action, suspended the right of habeas corpus, which permitted him to order the arrest and imprisonment of his political enemies without their having access to judicial relief. When confronted with constitutional objections to his action, Lincoln defended himself by saying that the Constitution was not "a suicide pact." The Supreme Court later held Lincoln's action unconstitutional.

After World War I and the Communist Revolution in Russia, a "Red scare" swept through the United States. President Woodrow Wilson's attorney general, A. Mitchell Palmer, became notorious in his zeal to protect the country's security. He conducted dragnet raids against aliens suspected of being communists or otherwise disloyal to the United States. These "Palmer Raids" resulted in wholesale imprisonment and deportation of aliens. This episode, too, is considered a shameful aberration in U.S. history, one an American government would never repeat.

Only it *was* repeated during a second "Red scare" that broke out after World War II. This time Congress was the offender, through the House Un-American Activities Committee and also in the person of Senator Joseph McCarthy. In their reckless and unscrupulous hunt for communists in government and other U.S. institutions, legislative officials, in the name of patriotism and security, falsely accused and ruined the reputations and lives of hundreds of loyal Americans. For a terrible period in the 1950s, a climate of fear occupied American life, particularly in Washington, D.C., where suspicion was rife and informers abounded. These abuses ended only when the leaders of Congress, President Eisenhower, and the U.S. news media revolted against them. This period, too, was an American embarrassment, viewed as the antithesis of how the United States should handle security problems.

As bad as these incidents were, the most shameful abuse of the liberty of citizens by American government occurred after the Japanese attack on Pearl Harbor on December 7, 1941, and the entry of the United States into the World War II against Japan and Germany the following day. At the time, 112,000 Japanese American citizens lived on the West Coast. Their presence suddenly frightened their embittered neighbors, who believed them to be potential, if not actual, supporters of our enemy Japan.

Without any evidence that these citizens were harmful to the country and without any resort to traditional procedures of American justice, President Franklin D. Roosevelt issued an executive order that authorized the army to seize and imprison in detention camps all of these Japanese Americans for the duration of hostilities. Whole families— men, women, and children—were uprooted from their homes and forcibly taken by the army to concentration camps, surrounded by barbed wire, in centrally located states.[1]

As the military commander of the Western Defense Command, Lieutenant General J. L. DeWitt issued the order excluding all Americans of Japanese ancestry from the West Coast and imprisoning them in camps. To General DeWitt, all Japanese Americans were "subversives," belonged to "an enemy race" whose "racial strains were undiluted," and constituted "over 112,000 potential enemies."[2] DeWitt later explained his actions against Americans of Japanese ancestry:

> I don't want any of them [Americans of Japanese ancestry] here. They are a dangerous element. There is no way to determine their loyalty. The west coast contains too many vital installations essential to the defense of the country to allow any Japanese on this coast. . . . The danger of the Japanese was, and is now—if they are permitted to come back—espionage and sabotage. It makes no difference whether he is an American citizen, he is still a Japanese. American citizenship does not necessarily determine loyalty. . . . But we must worry about the Japanese all the time until he is wiped off the map. Sabotage and espionage will make problems as long as he is allowed in this area.[3]

Fred Korematsu was twenty years old and working as a welder in the San Francisco shipyard at the time of General DeWitt's order. He was a U.S. citizen, born in California of Japanese parents who had emigrated to the United States. He had tried to join the U.S. Army but had been rejected for medical reasons. Korematsu had an Italian American girlfriend and did not want to leave his home to go to a prison camp as he was ordered. Besides, he could not understand why, as an American citizen, he had to. He considered himself and all his Japanese American friends to be loyal American citizens. He even tried to disguise his appearance by some botched plastic surgery.

Congress had made it a federal misdemeanor to disobey a military order such as the one General DeWitt had issued. Fred Korematsu was found by military police when he failed to report to the camp on time. He was arrested, tried, and convicted. His case reached the Supreme Court, which agreed to rule on the important constitutional issue of whether Japanese Americans could be singled out for removal to prison camps simply because the military authorities had determined they were a security risk on the West Coast during war with Japan.

The majority opinion, written by Justice Hugo Black, capitulated to the discretionary power of the president as commander-in-chief of the military in time of war.[4] Justice Black recognized that Japanese Americans had suffered discrimination and arbitrary imprisonment, but he concluded that in time of war, the Court did not have the competence to evaluate military security decisions.[5] Justice Frankfurter, who concurred with the majority opinion, brushed off Korematsu's treatment by the military somewhat flippantly by saying, "To find that the Constitution does not forbid the military measures now complained of does not carry with it approval of that which Congress and the Executive did. That is their business, not ours."

Three justices did think it was the Court's business and dissented strongly. They were Justices Roberts, Murphy, and Jackson. Justice Roberts criticized the majority for minimizing the case as simply a criminal violation of military orders and ignoring the essential nature of Korematsu's complaint. "[I]t is a case," he wrote, "of convicting a citizen as a punishment for not submitting to imprisonment in a concentration camp, based on his ancestry, and solely because of his ancestry, without evidence or inquiry concerning his loyalty and good disposition to the

United States." As so defined, Justice Roberts said, "I need hardly labor the conclusion that constitutional rights were violated." Justice Murphy agreed with Justice Roberts, declaring, "This exclusion of all persons of Japanese ancestry, both alien and non-alien . . . goes over the very brink of constitutional power and falls into the ugly abyss of racism."

Justice Jackson wondered how Korematsu could have been convicted of what is not "commonly a crime." He described his offense as "being present in the state whereof he is a citizen, near the place where he was born, and where all his life he had lived." Jackson pointed out that others of a different ancestry who did what Korematsu did would have been innocent of any crime. Korematsu's crime, Jackson wrote, resulted "not from anything he did, said, or thought different than they, but only in that he was born of different racial stock." Justice Jackson then reminded the majority of a basic principle of American law:

> Now, if any fundamental assumption underlies our system, it is that guilt is personal and not inheritable. Even if all of one's antecedents had been convicted of treason, the Constitution forbids its penalties to be visited upon him, for it provides that "no attainder of treason shall work corruption of blood, or forfeiture, except during the life of the person attained." But here is an attempt to make an otherwise innocent act a crime merely because this prisoner is the son of parents as to whom he had no choice, and belongs to a race from which there is no way to resign. If Congress in peace-time legislation should enact such a criminal law, I should suppose this Court would refuse to enforce it.[6]

In 1983, after many years of justice-seeking by Japanese Americans, Congress created the Federal Commission on War Time Relocation and Internment. The membership of the commission was made up of former congressmen and Supreme Court justices. The commission issued a report condemning the imprisonment of Japanese Americans in concentration camps and blamed the government's outrageous conduct on "broad prejudice, war hysteria, and a failure of political leadership." The commission concluded that the imprisonment was illegal and that "a grave injustice was done to American citizens and resident aliens of Japanese ancestry." The commission recommended that restitution be made to the survivors. In 1988, the Civil Liberties Act, awarding restitution, was passed by Congress and signed by President Ronald Reagan. The last of more than 80,000 payments, totaling $1.6 billion, were made early in the administration of President Bill Clinton.

In 1984, forty-two years after his arrest, Fred Korematsu finally succeeded in having his conviction vacated by means of the filing of the ancient writ of *coram nobis* in the U.S. District Court for the Northern District of California.[7] The federal government did not oppose Korematsu's request. In 1998, Fred Korematsu was awarded the Medal of Freedom by President Clinton for his courageous challenge to government injustice. The nation has now apologized to Korematsu and his fellow Japanese Americans for its violation of their rights. However, the survivors' emotional scars from their experience of indignity and humiliation will remain for the rest of their lives.

This brief history of senseless government abandonment of constitutional rights raises the question of why the government has repeatedly made these tragic mistakes. It is not as if these liberty restrictions were necessary or helpful to the government in keeping the country secure. None of them were. Rather, they were divisive and resulted in greater insecurity in the country. Oppression does not breed patriotism and loyalty.

Why, then does the government now follow the same erroneous strategy? As we have shown in previous chapters, the government's law enforcement powers are greater now than they have ever been. Why is the government seeking more power, and do government officials need it?

After 9/11, the president and his attorney general demanded greater search and seizure powers than a permissive Supreme Court had already given them. Though members of Congress grumbled, they submitted to these demands, desiring to appear as patriotic as the president in the war on terrorism. They enacted and the president signed Public Law 107–56, entitled the "Uniting and Strengthening America by Providing Appropriate Tools Required to Intercept and Obstruct Terrorism Act." The words of this awkward title were carefully put together to create a dissent-chilling acronym: the USA-PATRIOT Act.

The USA-PATRIOT Act dangerously eliminates a number of limitations Congress had previously placed on government surveillance of individuals, even in national security matters. Prior to 9/11, the Foreign Intelligence Surveillance Act, which permitted wiretapping and other forms of surveillance without the government having to show probable cause, was restricted to investigation of foreign spies. This broader power of surveillance was prohibited from use against American citizens, who were guaranteed the constitutional protections of the Fourth Amendment.

Under the new antiterror legislation, U.S. citizens lose their constitutional protection whenever federal law enforcement agents tell a federal judge that their investigation is relevant to foreign intelligence. The agents can then receive authority to wiretap the telephones of Americans and search their homes without having to comply with Fourth Amendment requirements of probable cause or particularly describing the thing or conversation to be seized or the place to be searched.

Worse yet, under this legislation, federal agents can sneak into the homes of Americans to obtain evidence without having to comply with the constitutional requirement of giving prior notice to the residents. All they have to do is tell the judge that giving notice would "impede their investigation." In ordinary criminal investigations, the Supreme Court has held that, under the Fourth Amendment, an officer with a warrant seeking to enter a home must first knock and announce his purpose, unless such notice would endanger the officer or lead to the imminent destruction of evidence. This requirement of notice is hallowed in ancient English law, which Sir Edward Coke, in the seventeenth century, claimed derived from the Magna Carta.

In addition, the Bush administration succeeded in getting Congress to give federal agents authority to engage in dragnet wiretapping and searches. Under prior law, the agent had to be able to specify a particular target person or telephone. In the war on terrorism, the government complained that they could not always do so. Under the USA-PATRIOT Act, federal agents can now obtain roving warrants, good for any suspected person, place, or telephone anywhere in the country.

Attorney General John Ashcroft's appetite for increased investigative power was not satisfied by what Congress gave him in the USA-PATRIOT Act. Alarming the public by his predictions of new terrorist attacks and decrying the impediments he claimed law enforcement agents confronted under existing legal restrictions, the attorney general set about giving himself additional powers without benefit of legislation. Ashcroft issued a federal regulation authorizing prison officials to intercept and record telephone conversations between detainees in custody on suspicion of terrorism and their lawyers without prior judicial authority.

While the courts have permitted the monitoring of general prisoner phone calls on the ground that prisoners can have no reasonable expectation of privacy during such calls, they have prohibited the monitoring of prisoner communications with lawyers.[8] These communications are protected by the Fourth Amendment and the attorney-client privilege. In reply to the American Bar Association's challenge to his actions, the attorney general explained that such recordings of attorney-client communications would only be made in a very few cases, and that he personally should be trusted to not misuse this power.

The fundamental principle upon which our constitutional protections are based is that powerful government officials cannot be so trusted. This concept is embodied in the oft-repeated statement of American judges that we are a government of law, not of men. James Madison illustrated this principle when he stated the following in *Federalist Papers 51*:

> If men were angels, no government would be necessary. If angels were to govern men, neither external or internal controls on government would be necessary. In framing a government which is to be administered by men over men, the great difficulty lies in this: you must first enable the government to control the governed; and in the next place to oblige it to control itself. A dependence on the people is no doubt the primary control on the government; but experience has taught mankind the necessity of auxiliary precautions.

An example of such uncontrolled government power occurred shortly after terrorists, who were Arabs, crashed their hijacked airliners into the World Trade Center, the Pentagon, and the Pennsylvania countryside. Federal agents arrested and imprisoned more than one thousand Arab and South Asian immigrants. These arrests were based on minor immigration violations, such as expired visas. The government defended imprisoning these terrorist-looking foreign men on the ground that they might be involved in terrorism or were material witnesses. The attorney general refused to identify these detainees or allow them to have open hearings.

In addition, more than five thousand legal Muslim immigrants, many of whom were students in U.S. universities, were notified that they would be interrogated by FBI agents. Although these interrogations were supposed to be voluntary, the agents were not told to inform the immigrants that they could refuse to be questioned without fear of retaliation. Most of the immigrants believed that they had to undergo interrogation or suffer some kind of punishment. The Muslim community in the United States was frightened, embittered, and discouraged by the government's associating them with terrorism simply because of their appearance and religion. It was reminiscent of the internment of Japanese Americans after the attack on Pearl Harbor.

This type of law enforcement racial profiling had outraged Americans in the past. Prior to 9/11, the victims of this treatment were mostly African Americans and Latino Americans. The crime of "driving while black" had become all too common on the highways of the United States. Law enforcement officers had been criticized for such practices, and government leaders had promised to put a stop to them.

Law enforcement racial profiling began with an effort by the Supreme Court to accommodate a bona fide law enforcement need. In 1968, the Supreme Court was asked by the state of Ohio, and the many other states that joined in the case, to authorize police to briefly stop and frisk persons on the street on the basis of the lesser standard of suspicion rather than probable cause, which controlled regular arrests and searches. The police argued that they needed this authorization to prevent serious felonies when they observed a person under circumstances giving them reasonable suspicion the person was about to commit a crime, although no crime had yet been committed.

Chief Justice Earl Warren, who had led the Court to strengthen Fourth Amendment protections, wrote the opinion in *Terry v. Ohio*,[9] which held that it was reasonable under the Fourth Amendment for a police officer to temporarily detain a citizen on the street and inquire into his conduct when the officer had reasonable suspicion that "crime is afoot." Warren rationalized that since these police street stops would occur anyway without much judicial control, it was better for the Court to recognize and regulate them. Justice Harlan added in his concurring opinion that when an officer reasonably suspected the person was about to commit a felony, the officer should be able not only to seize that person temporarily and make an inquiry but also to immediately pat down the person's clothing to determine if he was armed with a weapon, so that the answer to his inquiry "will not be a bullet."

This well-meaning effort of the Court to dilute Fourth Amendment requirements in the interest of preventing major crime has encouraged law enforcement officers to broaden their intrusion into the ordinary private lives of citizens. Random street stops and frisks, mostly of African American men in urban neighborhoods, have been common under the guise of drug enforcement. Cars are routinely stopped in such areas under the pretext of a broken taillight or the nervous reaction of a nonwhite driver at the sight of a patrol car.

The Supreme Court has upheld this unreasonably intrusive police action on the basis of any slight technically supported excuse of the police, ruling out any consideration of the actual improper motives of the officers involved. The Court's majority has appeared to be insensitive to the personal humiliation and degradation of the people treated this way by the police. These cases have detoured a great distance from the reasoning of *Terry v. Ohio* and have made the principles of that case practically unrecognizable. They also have persuaded the attorney general that he is justified in authorizing the sweeping up of Muslim immigrants and detaining them in prison.

The attorney general has also sought to launch two other dragnet strategies to identify potential terrorists. In doing so, he has either forgotten or ignored similar abusive government investigative practices of the past that were exposed by Congress and brought shame and censure on the FBI and other government intelligence agencies.

In a totalitarian state where individual freedom has been snuffed out, the attorney general's plans would have a simple logic.

He has authorized federal agents to infiltrate houses of worship, social meetings, and other gatherings of American citizens to detect any sign of potential terrorist activity. The attorney general claims that if the public can attend such gatherings, an FBI agent also should be able to attend, even in the absence of any proof of wrongdoing. Logical? Yes, but this logic is completely divorced from any basic understanding of the tradition and history of freedom and individual liberty in the United States and of what constitutional restrictions on government action are all about.

The plan also ignores common sense and the pervasive fear that would threaten the free assembly of Americans, whether in houses of worship or social gatherings. We value free expression of ideas in our democracy, which is encouraged and protected by our Constitution. However, in a time of suspicion and fear, the public's knowledge that FBI agents may be present at its meetings would surely chill, if not suffocate, free expression.

The attorney general has offered a parallel plan to identify potential terrorists that is equally insensitive to American values. He wants to create a nationwide network of private informers under a program called TIPS (Terrorism Information and Prevention System). Under this plan, mail carriers, meter readers, and others who have access to private homes would be asked to watch for signs of potential terrorists and report them to federal agents. The attorney general has asked all Americans to watch their neighbors and report suspicious activity. This proposal received such nationwide protest and criticism that the attorney general was forced to partially abandon it.

By proposing his dragnet program to spy on Americans in their churches, political and social organizations, and homes, the attorney general was resurrecting a previously disgraced domestic intelligence operation of the FBI that, when exposed, was rejected by Congress and despised by the American people. During the "Red scare" of the 1950s and 1960s, J. Edgar Hoover initiated his secret counterintelligence program—labeled in FBI files as "Cointelpro."[10] Under this program, FBI agents were assigned to infiltrate the American Indian Movement (AIM), the Communist Party, the Social Workers' Party, Black Nationalist groups, antiwar groups, numerous civil rights groups such as antiracist groups and feminist, lesbian, and gay organizations, and environmentalist groups. Cointelpro also targeted many other groups and individuals seeking racial, gender, and class justice, including Martin Luther King Jr., Cesar Chavez, the NAACP, the

National Lawyers' Guild, and the American Friends Service Committee. This dark period of FBI domestic intelligence operations came to light when, in 1971, an anonymous Citizens' Committee to Investigate the FBI sponsored a burglary of the FBI offices in Media, Pennsylvania, during which the burglars removed secret files that provided detailed information about Cointelpro. After these files were released to the press, agents began resigning from the FBI and blowing the whistle on Cointelpro covert operations.[11] None of the burglars or members of the committee were ever identified or caught. It was presumed that those involved were part of a group opposed to the Vietnam War.

It was during this same period that President Richard Nixon unlawfully authorized the FBI to wiretap and bug the telephones and conversations of U.S. citizens who dissented from his Vietnam War program. In addition, after Daniel Ellsberg stole the "Pentagon Papers" and released them to the press, Nixon developed a band of burglars and wiretappers working out of the White House to discredit Ellsberg and other whistleblowers. Nixon's leak snoopers were called the "Plumbers." The Senate Watergate Committee exposed these illegal White House activities in public hearings in 1973.

In 1975, the Senate Select Committee on Intelligence Activities, chaired by Senator Frank Church, conducted an extensive investigation and public hearings on the domestic intelligence activities of the FBI, the CIA, the National Security Agency, and Army Intelligence. The hearings exposed to the American public the flagrant civil rights violations of J. Edgar Hoover's Cointelpro. Congress and the Department of Justice promised reforms.

The most significant reform came in the form of the domestic intelligence guidelines created by the Department of Justice. They were ordered by Attorney General Edward Levi, former president of the University of Chicago, who had been appointed by President Gerald Ford after the Watergate exposures to win back the public's confidence

in federal law enforcement. Uppermost in these guidelines was the prohibition of federal agents interfering with the activities of U.S. citizens
or their social, religious, and political organizations unless there was a
reasonable basis to believe federal criminal violations were being committed.

Although the Levi Guidelines were somewhat loosened during
the administration of President Ronald Reagan and afterward, they
continued to require that agents have a reasonable suspicion of federal
organization or group. Congress's continuing concern over federal
agents' unrestricted infiltration into social or political action groups was
emphasized in the 1989 report of the Senate Select Committee on
Intelligence Activities concerning its investigation of the FBI infiltration of CISPES (Committee in Solidarity with the People of El
Salvador). The report stated:

> The American people have the right to disagree with the poli-
> cies of their government, to support unpopular political causes,
> and to associate with others in peaceful expression of those
> views, without fear of investigation by the FBI or any other
> government agency. As Justice Lewis Powell wrote in the *Keith*
> case, "The price of lawful public dissent must not be a dread of
> subjection to an unchecked surveillance power." . . .
> Unjustified investigations of political expression and dissent
> can have a debilitating effect upon our political system. When
> people see that this can happen, they become wary of associat-
> ing with groups that disagree with the government and more
> wary of what they say and write. The impact is to undermine
> the effectiveness of popular self-government. If the people are
> inhibited in expressing their views, a nation's government
> becomes increasingly divorced from the will of its citizens.[12]

Attorney General Ashcroft has abandoned caution and safeguards
and has adopted the rejected and discredited tactics of J. Edgar Hoover's
Cointelpro by authorizing federal agents to engage in dragnet infiltration
of innocent private organizations and groups without having any reason

to believe that there has been or is about to be any violation of federal criminal law.

The attorney general's new domestic intelligence program seeks to reassure us that FBI spies will not misuse information they obtain in this way because he has ordered that such information not be disseminated to law enforcement agents unless it is related to a violation of federal criminal law. However, this is no protection at all. The attorney general misses the point of why the nation rejected Cointelpro. The harm to free expression, free worship, and free dissent has already been done by the federal agent's unsupported presence as a government spy.

More recently, as a new method to determine who among us in America are terrorists, the Pentagon proudly announced a plan called Total Information Awareness to develop a database on the private lives of all Americans. Worse, put in charge of this new operation was former admiral John Poindexter, notorious for having been convicted by a federal criminal trial jury for lying to Congress about the illegal arms-for-hostages secret plan of the Reagan administration, known as Iran/Contra.[13] As first announced, Poindexter said the plan would cull information from telephone records, credit card purchases, gun purchases, arrests, rental car records, airline reservations, medical files, education reports, and many other files and records covering millions of Americans.

Poindexter resigned his Pentagon position after Congress, which has been complacently giving way to other restrictions on liberty, balked at this one. In an appropriations bill, it scuttled the Pentagon plan and barred further action on it by the executive branch without prior consultation with Congress. The *Hartford Courant* editorialized, "The Orwellian proposal, coined Total Information Awareness, was devised by John Poindexter, the navy rear admiral who helped create a plan in the 1980's to illegally send money to Nicaraguan rebels. . . . Many lawmakers were justifiably outraged at the implications of an extensive data base on every American."[14]

Put together, these sweeping new investigative powers initiated by the federal government are nothing short of frightening and are clearly incompatible with a free society—even in a time of crisis involving the security of the country. Reasonable people can and do differ on how much freedom we as Americans should surrender in time of war or war-like conditions. Most agree that certain restrictions can be tolerated without losing the basic quality of constitutional liberty. However, the determination of its necessity and efficacy must be at the heart of any such restriction.

Do federal law enforcement officers really need these expanded powers to engage in effective investigations and prosecutions of terrorists in our midst? There is ample evidence that they do not. Congressional investigations into how our intelligence agencies and the Department of Justice failed to be more prepared for the terrorist attacks on 9/11 point more to incompetence than lack of investigative powers or resources. The strong arsenal of federal law enforcement investigative powers—all granted by Congress and the Supreme Court to law enforcement agencies prior to the attorney general's demand for expanded powers—has been shown to fully allow competent law enforcement officers and prosecutors to successfully protect the country's security against criminal extremists and terrorists.

Professor Philip B. Heymann of Harvard Law School has persuasively demonstrated this capability of law enforcement agencies under the laws and investigative powers existing before 9/11. His book *Terrorism and America* was published in 1998, three years before 9/11, but it is a prophetic manual for meeting the enforcement problems of 9/11 terrorism today. Heymann served as assistant attorney general, chief of the criminal division of the U.S. Department of Justice, during the Jimmy Carter administration and as deputy attorney general, the number-two spot at Justice, during the Clinton administration.

Heymann illustrates his claim that law enforcement officials have sufficient powers under existing law to investigate and prosecute terrorists by describing the successful investigation of the bombing of the World Trade Center in 1993. The investigation, he writes, started at the crime scene, in the crater that the bomb had created, with an army of meticulous searchers. The agents and officers talked to witnesses as quickly as they could be located. Hotlines were immediately established, and rewards were offered. Police were asked to tell the agents of any arrests or traffic stops near the time of the explosion. Agents checked whether there had been any threatening calls or any other messages that might hold clues.

A wider search for evidence involved a review of all recorded information from the pay phones in the area, from all the security video cameras scanning the area at banks and other businesses, and from intelligence and law enforcement agencies that might have picked up something that could be helpful. Heymann describes how the agents checked with informants and carefully reviewed tapes looking for clues of any past electronic surveillance by groups that might have been responsible. Any physical evidence that might have helped was sent immediately to FBI laboratories and was promptly processed. This meticulous collection of evidence led to the discovery of a tiny scrap of the rented vehicle that was enough of a lead to enable the FBI to trace the vehicle to a rental agency, ultimately opening up the leads to identify the bombers. "The case was solved," Heymann writes, "by an intensive use of familiar investigative techniques." He concludes,

> It is obvious from the success of the World Trade Center investigation and of the related investigation of the conspiracy to bomb other sites in the New York area, the conviction of Timothy McVeigh for bombing the federal building in Oklahoma City, and the capture of the "Unabomber," Theodore Kaczynski, that the United States has been able to find evidence and prosecute terrorists' bombings under existing rules for investigation and trial. In each case, massive resources have been directed to the solution of the crimes, but it has not been necessary to change the rules.[15]

This same conclusion can be made concerning the arrests and prosecutions since 9/11 of persons connected in some way to the al Qaeda terrorists. None of the expanded powers of surveillance, searches, or investigations acquired by the attorney general were needed. Yet the existence of these powers and their threatened use by law enforcement officials have created an atmosphere of fear and suspicion throughout the country and have doubtless had a chilling effect on free expression of ideas and dissent among the people.

If the goal of the terrorists is, as President Bush has declared, to destroy the United States as a free and democratic nation, then the federal government's panicked rush to needlessly restrict the liberties of American citizens has provided the terrorists with a victory. A successful war on the terrorists requires quite the opposite strategy. The United States must show the terrorists that the liberty and freedom of its people are its impregnable shield and sword. These essential qualities of a free society have enabled us to flourish economically as a powerful nation and militarily as an invincible champion of democracy.

The wonderful thing about this challenge is that we do not have to create anything—we already have it. Freedom is our heritage from the birth of our nation. It is inscribed in our living Constitution that was so bravely created and has so miraculously endured.

As a people who are the ultimate sovereign in America, we must insist that our government leaders reflect our pride and trust in the American values of liberty and freedom. Our leaders should protect them and rely on them, rather than distrust them as not strong enough to preserve American security. Our government leaders—executive, legislative, and judicial branches—have made many mistakes in the past when they have lost sight of the sacred American values rooted in the Declaration of Independence and the Constitution. We are at the brink of even graver mistakes and assaults on these values. We dare not turn away from them—for how naked, weak, and poor we will be without them.

Notes

PROLOGUE

1. Records of the Select Committee on Presidential Campaign Activities 1973, 1974, *Senate Watergate Hearings*, National Archives.

2. Statement of Philadelphia Police Commissioner Frank Rizzo to author, telephone conversation, Washington, D.C., 1967.

3. Copies of correspondence in author's possession between Judge David L. Bazelon and Attorney General Nicholas DeB. Katzenbach, June 1965.

4. Genesis 19:4–11.

5. Genesis 31:11–35. The fact that Laban declined to disturb Rachel can be attributed to her being untouchable as unclean during her claimed menstrual period or to a sensitivity against searching the person. This immunity from personal search is reflected later in English law in Ward's Case (1636) Clay 44, cited in David Feldman, *The Law Relating to Entry, Search, and Seizure* (Oxford: Butterworth, 1986), 4. In that case, a constable searching a house for stolen goods under a warrant attempted to search under the dress of a woman in bed in the house. The court held that this conduct rendered the search invalid.

6. Joshua 2:1–7.

7. Joshua 7:10–26.

8. Another such example is found in Deuteronomy 24:10–11. "When you make a loan to another man, do not enter his house to take a pledge from him. Wait outside, and the man whose creditor you are shall bring the pledge out to you."

9. Article 21, Code of Hammurabi.

10. Justinian 1, D. 50, 17, 103, cited in Max Rabin, *Handbook on Roman Law* (St. Paul, Minn.: West Publishing, 1927).

11. In ancient Rome, there were no public prosecutors. Both civil suits and criminal cases were prosecuted by private complainants. A private complainant alleging that X stole his property was required to particularly describe to a judicial officer the property and the place where it was kept. The court would grant the complainant authority to enter X's house to search for the property and to seize it if it were found there. However, the Roman court imposed a peculiar legal ceremony on the searcher aimed at preventing him from incriminating an innocent person by planting the property in his home. The complainant had to carry an empty platter and be dressed only in an apron. He was accompanied by witnesses and a court bailiff.

CHAPTER 1. THE LEGEND OF THE MAGNA CARTA

1.   Charles Henry Browning, *The Magna Charta Barons and Their American Descendants Together with the Pedigrees of the Founders of the Order of Runnemede Deduced* (Baltimore: Genealogical Researchers Publishing, 1969), 94.

2.   Geoffrey Hindley, *The Book of Magna Carta* (London: Constable, 1990), 166.

3.   A. J. Robertson, *The Laws of the Kings of England from Edmond to Henry I* (Cambridge: The University Press, 1925), 283.

4.   James Clarke Holt, ed. *Magna Carta and the Idea of Liberty* (Melbourne, Fla.: Krieger, 1982), 51.

5.   Helen M. Cam, *Magna Carta—Event or Document?*, Seldon Society Lecture (London: Bernard Quaritch, 1965), 11.

6.   Sir Edward Coke, *Institutes*, Cap. 31, Section 178; Cap. 73, Section 162 ([London] In the Savoy: E. and R. Nutt, and R. Gosling, 1725).

7.   9 Ed. III Ca. 9–11; 2 Henry VIII Ca. 27; Eliz. I Ca. 13, renewing Henry VIII statute.

8.   26 Henry VIII, c. I; I Elizabeth, c. S. Viii; in Roland G. Usher, *The Rise and Fall of the High Commission* (Oxford: Clarendon Press, 1969).

9.   Ibid., 27–28.

10.   The terror the commission's sweeping general searches caused Catholic families is evidenced by a remarkable find in the mid-eighteenth century. In 1757, a builder remodeling an old house in Stratford-upon-Avon found several fastened pages of old handwriting hidden in the roof rafters. The house was none other than the one that had belonged to John Shakespeare, father of the great bard William Shakespeare. The house had been William's birthplace, and at the time of the discovery, a distant relative was still living in it. The writing on the pages professed to be the testament of John Shakespeare. Later research on these handwritten pages showed that it was a copy of the Catholic testaments the Jesuits had surreptitiously distributed to secret Catholic families. Ian Wilson, *Shakespeare: the Evidence: Unlocking the Mysteries of the Man and His Work* (New York: St. Martin's Press, 1994), 44–58.

11.   Catherine Drinker Bowen, *John Adams and the American Revolution* (New York: Little, Brown, 1950), 301–306.

12.   Hastings Lyon and Herman Block, *Edward Coke: Oracle of the Law* (1929; reprint, Littleton, Colo.: Fred B. Rothman, 1992), 327.

13.   Bowen, *John Adams*, 493–494.

14.   Cuthbert W. Johnson, *Life of Sir Edward Coke* (London: 1837), cited in Nelson Bernard Lasson, *The History and Development of the Fourth Amendment to the United States Constitution* (Baltimore: Johns Hopkins University Press, 1937), 31.

15. Morris Ashley, *Magna Carta in the Seventeenth Century* (Charlottesville: University Press of Virginia, 1995), 3.
16. Richard L. Perry and John L. Cooper, *Sources of Our Liberties* (Chicago: American Bar Foundation, 1959), 1.
17. Johnson, *Life of Sir Edward Coke*, cited in Lasson, *The History and Development of the Fourth Amendment*, 39.

CHAPTER 2. WILKES AND LIBERTY

1. R. W. Postgate, *That Devil Wilkes* (New York: Vanguard Press, 1929).
2. Ibid., 48–49.
3. Ibid., 51.
4. Ibid., 52.
5. John Wilkes, *A Complete Collection of the Genuine Papers, Letters, etc. in the Case of John Wilkes, Esq.* (London: Berlin, 1769).
6. Ibid., 2.
7. Ibid., 5.
8. Ibid., 6–7.
9. Ibid., 18–19.
10. Ibid., 38
11. Ibid., 30–32.
12. Postgate, *That Devil Wilkes*, 53–57.
13. Wilkes, *Collection*, 38–39.
14. Postgate, *That Devil Wilkes*, 50.
15. Ibid.
16. Ibid.
17. Wilkes, *Collection*, 33–34.
18. Ibid., 34–35
19. Henry S. Eeles, *Lord Chancellor Camden and His Family* (London: Philip Allan, 1934), 70.
20. 2 Wills. K.B. 274 (1765)
21. Eeles, *Lord Chancellor Camden*, 70.
22. *Entick v. Carrington*, 2 Wills. K.B. 274, 289 (1765)
23. Ibid., 282.
24. Ibid., 282–283.
25. Eeles, *Lord Chancellor Camden*, 75.
26. Wilkes, *Collection*, 204–205.
27. Eeles, *Lord Chancellor Camden*, 72–73.
28. Postgate, *That Devil Wilkes*, 82–83.
29. Ibid., 88–89.
30. Ibid., 98.
31. Eeles, *Lord Chancellor Camden*, 130–131.
32. Ibid., 132.

33. Wilkes, *Collection*, 222–223.
34. Postgate, *That Devil Wilkes*, 136–137.
35. Ibid., 138; Wilkes, *Collection*, 227.

CHAPTER 3. A FLAME OF FIRE

1. M. H. Smith, *The Writs of Assistance Case* (Berkeley and Los Angeles: University of California Press, 1978).
2. William Tudor, *Life of James Otis of Massachusetts* (Boston: Wells and Lilly, 1823), 53.
3. Ibid., 54–55.
4. Ibid., 53–54.
5. Ibid.
6. Ibid., 53 n.
7. Catherine Drinker Bowen, *John Adams and the American Revolution* (New York: Little, Brown, 1950), 212.
8. Tudor, *Life of James Otis*, 61.
9. Bowen, *John Adams*, 214.
10. J. Galvin, *Three Men of Boston Passion* (New York: Crowell, 1976), 39–40, quoted in 26 *American Criminal Law Review* 1397 (1989): 1400.
11. Smith, *The Writs of Assistance Case*, 497.
12. *American Criminal Law Review*, 1403.
13. Even stranger, the Declaration of Independence in its list of grievances against George III did not include any reference to the hated writs of assistance and general search warrants. This omission must have been an oversight, since John Adams, who believed the dragnet searches imposed on the colonists by the Crown sparked the Revolution, worked closely with Thomas Jefferson in planning the content of the Declaration and in closely reviewing Jefferson's draft.
14. Bernard Lasson, *The History and Development of the Fourth Amendment to the United States Constitution* (Baltimore: Johns Hopkins University Press, 1937), 83–90.
15. Jonathan Elliot, ed., *The Debates on the Federal Constitution III* (1836), 441–445.
16. John A. Jameson, *The Constitutional Convention* (Chicago: E. B. Myers, 1869); Lasson, *History and Development of the Fourth Amendment*, 97.
17. William C. Rives, *History of the Life and Times of James Madison*, vol. 3 (Boston: 1873), 40–44; Lasson, *History and Development of the Fourth Amendment*, 98–100.
18. John B. McMaster and Frederick D. Stone, *Pennsylvania and the Federal Constitution, 1787–1788* (Philadelphia: Pennsylvania Historical Society, 1888).
19. Elliot, ed., *Debates*, 468.

20. Lasson, *History and Development of the Fourth Amendment.*
21. Article XIV of the Massachusetts Declaration declared:

> Every subject has a right to be secure from all unreasonable searches and seizures of his person, his house, his papers and of all his possessions. All warrants, therefore, are contrary to this right, if the cause or foundation of them be not previously supported by oath or affirmation, and if the order in the warrant to a civil officer, to make search in suspected places, or to arrest one or more suspected persons, or to seize their property, be not accompanied with a special designation of the person or objects of the search, arrest or seizure.

22. Lasson, *History and Development of the Fourth Amendment,* 81.
23. U.S. Congress, *Annals of Congress,* 1st Cong., 1st sess., 1789, p. 783.
24. Ibid., 452
25. U.S. Congress, *House Journal,* 1st Cong., 1st Sess., 24 August 1789.
26. Professor Akhil Reed Amar labels this history a "widespread canard" in his article, "Fourth Amendment First Principles," 107 *Harvard Law Review* 757 (1994): 775, footnote 66. He speculates that Benson's draft may have been approved initially and is the draft of the Fourth Amendment that the Congress wanted to adopt. However, his claim is unsupported by any proof other than his guesswork and fails even to mention Madison's draft, which was approved and which destroys the central argument of his article that the framers did not prefer that searches be made on warrants based on probable cause.
27. Ibid. Professor Amar is the leading proponent of this view. His article is long, and it would take an equally long article to refute him. However, I believe I can deal with his main points here. First, he relies on common law history and claims there is no support there for the requirement of a search or seizure warrant based on probable cause. To the contrary, he interprets the common law as being hostile to warrants, particularly because warrants were issued by government officials and immunized the sheriff or the constable from a civil suit for damages before a jury. Amar then divines the "intention" of the framers of the Fourth Amendment, which he states, without any citation to any of the debates of the framers or to any other source, as disfavoring warrants based on probable cause and preferring that the standard for lawful searches be simply reasonableness to be determined by civil juries in damage suits. Amar's common law history is faulty. There are no common law cases that define "reasonableness" as the standard for a lawful search or that prefer jury trials against offending officers to determining the reasonableness of a search or seizure. Amar says that there is very little said in the common law treatises written by Coke, Blackstone, Hale, or Hawkins about the requirement for a warrant based on probable cause to make a search or a seizure

lawful. He is wrong. The common law commentators all emphasized the need for such a warrant. William Blackstone, *Commentaries on the Law of England, A Facsimile of the First Edition of 1765–1769* (Chicago: University of Chicago Press, 1979), chapter 21; William Hawkins, *A Treatise of the Pleas of the Crown* (New York: Garland, 1721), 84; Matthew Hale, *Historia Placitorum Coronae: The History of Pleas of the Crown* (1728), vol. 11 (in the Savoy [London]: E. and R. Nutt and R. Gosling, 1736), 110–113, 150. Each of these commentators declared that general warrants were illegal. Perhaps the leading authority on this subject in the common law was Sir Edward Coke, who was cited by Blackstone, Hawkins, and Hale. In Part 11, Magna Carta, 52; Part 4, *Justices of the Peace*, 177, of his *Institutes*, Coke repeatedly emphasized the need for a warrant based on probable cause to render a search or seizure lawful. It was Coke's claim that a warrant "on bare surmise" (without probable cause) was unlawful that led the later commentators to state that general warrants were illegal. Despite these pronouncements by the commentators, general warrants were frequently used and upheld. Indeed the writs of assistance, which were the most general of warrants, were still lawful in England at the time of the American Revolution. It was precisely to guarantee that such general warrants would not be used in the newly freed nation that the Fourth Amendment was drafted. In this regard, Professor Amar's repeated reliance on the Wilkes line of cases decided by Lord Camden in the mid-eighteenth century is misplaced. The court's holding in those cases was that the warrants were unlawful because the secretary of state did not have jurisdiction to issue them, not that searches without warrants at all might have been reasonable in this case. In addition, those were jury trials in which the messengers of the secretary of state were not immunized because they had warrants. Here, again, Amar misreads the common law. His claim that the immunity officials received from civil jury suits for damages when they obtained a warrant led the framers to be hostile to warrants is unfounded. At common law, officials were immunized from civil liability only when the warrant was a lawful one, as they should have been. There is no evidence, and Amar produces none, that the framers were troubled with this. Amar also wrongly argues that the fact that at common law some arrests and searches could be made without a warrant supports his argument that warrants were not a requirement. Such exceptions were based on necessity at common law and under the search and seizure law of this country and reaffirm the requirement of a warrant based on probable cause in the ordinary case, rather than prove that such warrants were not required at all. Finally, the framers were not hostile to warrants, as Amar speculates. Their experience under English rule led them to dislike government searches and seizures, and they sought to guarantee, through the Fourth Amendment, that it would be difficult for the government to engage in them as a result of their strict requirements of warrants based on probable cause, particularly describing the place to be searched and the thing to be seized.

28. *Coolidge v. New Hampshire*, 403 U.S. 443 (1971).

29. *Silverman v. United States*, 3 U.S. 55 (1961).

30. Professor Amar disputes this conclusion, claiming the framers wanted the standard for a lawful search to be simply whether it was reasonable and preferred to allow a civil jury to determine whether it was or not. There is certainly no evidence that this was the framers' intention. To the contrary, the evidence demonstrates that the framers wanted to prohibit the use of general warrants by requiring special warrants based on probable cause. Moreover, Amar's enchantment with civil juries providing money damages for criminal defendants who are victims of unlawful searches and seizures is at best completely naive today and ignores the finding in *Mapp v. Ohio* that civil suits are worthless as a remedy for violations of the Fourth Amendment. This is what compelled the court to rely on the exclusionary rule as the only viable remedy. Whatever willingness an English jury had in the eighteenth century to give substantial damages to the popular and heroic figure John Wilkes, today a U.S. civil jury would be loath to favor a convicted drug peddler on whom the drugs were actually found, though unlawfully, with damages against the drug enforcement officer who seized the drugs.

CHAPTER 4. THE PLATE-GLASS DUTY FRAUD CASE

1. Of course, one reason was that the Supreme Court was not given appellate jurisdiction by Congress until after the Civil War.

2. *Frisbie v. Butler*, Conn. 1787, Kirby 213.

3. *Sandford v. Nicholas*, 13 Mass. 286 (Mass. 1816).

4. *Banks v. Farewell*, 21 Pick. 156 (Middlesex 1838).

5. *Boyd v. U.S.*, Oct. Term 1885, No. 983, Record 12.

6. Ibid., Brief for Plaintiff 2.

7. Ibid.

8. Ibid., Record 23–24.

9. Ibid.

10. *Boyd*, Brief for the U.S. 4.

11. 116 U.S. 616 (1886).

12. There may be a Fourth Amendment issue with a subpoena if the subpoena is overly broad so as to be the equivalent of a general warrant.

CHAPTER 5. THE EXCLUSIONARY RULE

1. The courts distinguished at times between evidence obtained by means of an unlawful search and seizure and evidence obtained by government agents by means of other unlawful conduct, such as a coerced confession. It was readily recognized that a confession coerced from the accused would not be reliable and probative and should not be admitted as evidence.

2. *People v. Defore*, 242 N.Y.13

3. "The Lottery Here Again," *Kansas City Star*, 22 December 1911, p. 1.

4. Ibid.

5. The confusion produced by Boyd's treating the subpoenaed document as a seizure under the Fourth Amendment and then applying the Fifth Amendment conjointly with the Fourth continued a number of years after Weeks. In three subsequent cases, the Court ruled that both the Fourth and the Fifth Amendments required the exclusion of evidence obtained by means of an unlawful search and seizure. *Silverthorn v. U.S.*, 251 U.S. 385 (1920); *Gouled v. U.S.*, 255 U.S. 298 (1921); *Agnello v. U.S.*, 269 U.S. 20 (1925). By 1976, the Court had abandoned relying on the Fifth Amendment for excluding illegally seized evidence and based the exclusionary rule solely on the requirements of the Fourth Amendment. *Andresen v. Maryland*, 427 U.S. 463 (1976).

6. In doing so, it would have a problem explaining the function of the due process clause in the Fifth Amendment, which would then merely duplicate the other provisions of the Bill of Rights.

7. 302 U.S. 319 (1937).

8. 211 U.S. 78 (1908).

9. 332 U.S. 46 (1947).

10. 342 U.S. 165 (1952).

11. 338 U.S. 25 (1949).

12. *Wolf v. Colorado*, Oct. Term 1947, No. 18, Opp. Brief, R. 842.

13. Ibid.

CHAPTER 6. THE CASE OF THE "WHISPERING WIRES"

1. "Eleven Rum Defendants Are Taken Into Custody," *Seattle Daily Times*, 18 November 1924, p. 1.

2. "U.S. Raid on Olmsted Attorney's Office," *Seattle Daily Times*, 23 November 1924, p. 1; "'Bedtime' Stories Interrupted," *Seattle Daily Times*, 23 November 1924, p.13.

3. "Must Prove Bedtime Stories Were Not Bootleg Signals," *New York Times*, 30 November 1924, p. 1.

4. "Seattle Rum King to Have Rehearing," *New York Times*, 1 April 1928, p. 1.

5. Ibid.

6. *Olmstead v. U.S.*, Brief for the United States, p. 4

7. "Evidence from Tapped Telephones Carried Little Weight in Olmsted Case," *Seattle Daily Times*, 21 February 1926, p. 1.

8. "Attorney Is First to Surrender to Court," *Seattle Daily Times*, 20 January 1925, p. 1.

9. "Arguments of Defense Attorneys Are Heard," *Seattle Daily Times*, 19

February 1926, p. 1.
10. "Four Years and $8,000 Back of This Smile," *Seattle Daily Times*, 9 March 1926, p. 1.
11. "Rum King Chief Tells of Jones Fund Gift," *New York Times*, 23 August 1930, p. 1.
12. Cal. Stats., p. 288; Cal. Gen. Laws act 8530 (Deering 1944).
13. *Sacramento Daily Union*, 12 August 1864, p. 2, col. 4, as cited in Samuel Dash, *The Eavesdroppers* (New Brunswick: Rutgers University Press, 1959), 23.
14. Heros Von Borcke, *Memoirs of the Confederate War for Independence* (1866; reprint, Nashville, Tenn.: J. S. Sanders, 1999).
15. *San Francisco Call*, 1 January 1899, p. 3, as cited in Dash, *The Eavesdroppers*, 25.
16. Ibid.
17. *New York Times*, 18 May 1916, p. 1, col. 1, as cited in Dash, *The Eavesdroppers*, 25.
18. *New York Times*, 19 April 1916, p. 4, col. 2, as cited in Dash, *The Eavesdroppers*, 26.
19. *New York Times*, 27 May 1916, p. 3, col. 6, as cited in Dash, *The Eavesdroppers*, 26.
20. 48 Stat. 1103 (1934); 47 U.S.C. §605.
21. N.Y. Consol. Laws Ann., *Code of Criminal Procedures* § 813a (McKinney, 1944).
22. *Benanti v. United States*, 355 U.S. 96 (1957).
23. 316 U.S. 129 (1942).
24. Ibid.
25. *On Lee v. United States*, 343 U.S. 747 (1952).
26. *United States v. On Lee*, 201 F.2d 722 (2d Circuit 1953).
27. Dash, *The Eavesdroppers*.
28. Ibid., 95.
29. Ibid., 96.
30. Ibid., 212.
31. Ibid.
32. *Silverman v. United States*, 365 U.S. 505 (1961).
33. Dash, *The Eavesdroppers*, 367–371.
34. Ibid.
35. *Silverman v. United States*, 365 U.S. 505 (1961).
36. *Katz v. United States*, 389 U.S. 347 (1967).
37. 18 U.S.C.A. §2518 et seq.
38. *Scott v. United States*, 436 U.S 128 (1978).
39. 338 U.S. 25 (1949).
40. *Schwartz v. Texas*, 344 U.S. 199 (1952).

CHAPTER 7. DOLLY MAPP

1. "Archie Moore Suits Dismissed," *Cleveland Plain Dealer*, 2 April 1957, p. 3.
2. Don King went on to achieve great fame as a boxing promoter.
3. James Neff, "Searchers Unleashed," *Cleveland Plain Dealer*, 9 July 1984, editorial page, B-1.
4. Ibid.
5. Ibid.
6. Potter Stewart, "The Road to *Mapp v. Ohio* and Beyond: The Origin, Development and Future of the Exclusionary Rule in Search-and-Seizure Cases," 83 *Columbia Law Review* 1365 (1983).
7. Ironically, in *Stanley v. Georgia*, 334 U.S. 557 (1969), Justice Stewart castigated the majority for deciding the case on the First Amendment issue, which was raised by the petitioner, and not deciding the case on the Fourth Amendment issue, which was not raised by the petitioner.
8. "State Prosecutors Will Fight U.S. Curbs on Illegal Evidence," *New York Times*, 2 July 1961, p. 24.
9. Robert D. McFadden, "Figure in Landmark Case Is Seized Here as a Fence," *New York Times*, 3 November 1970, p. 24.
10. "Woman in Drug Case Gets Two Years to Life," *New York Times*, 27 May 1971, p. 1.
11. "16 Prisoners' Sentences Are Commuted by Carey," *New York Times*, 1 January 1981, p. 23.

CHAPTER 8. SMOTHERING THE FLAME

1. 403 U.S. 388 (1971).
2. 414 U.S. 338 (1974).
3. 428 U.S. 433 (1976).
4. Ibid.
5. 251 U.S. 385 (1920).
6. See Paul M. Bator, "Finality in Criminal Law and Federal Habeas Corpus in State Prison," *Harvard Law Review* 441 (1963): 76.
7. 362 U.S. 257 (1960).
8. 439 U.S. 128 (1978).
9. 389 U.S. 347 (1967).
10. *Minnesota v. Carter*, 525 U.S. 83 (1998).
11. *Minnesota v. Olson*, 495 U.S. 91 (1990).
12. See *Florida v. Riley*, 488 U.S. 445 (1989); *Dow Chemical Co. v. United States*, 476 U.S. 227 (1986).
13. 533 U.S. 27 (2001).

14.   468 U.S. 897 (1984).
15.   *Illinois v. Krull*, 480 U.S. 340 (1987).

CHAPTER 9. WAR ON TERROR: SECURITY AND LIBERTY

1.   For a detailed description of the Japanese internment during World War II see "Stories of Fourth Amendment Disrespect: From Elian to the Internment," *Fordham Law Review* 70 (2001): 2257, 2302–2316.
2.   Dissenting opinion of Justice Murphy, *Korematsu v. United States*, 323 U.S. 214, 233 (1944).
3.   Ibid.
4.   *Korematsu v. United States*, 323 U.S. 214 (1944).
5.   On the same day the Court decided Korematsu, it ordered the release of Mitsuye Endo on habeas corpus from the Central Utah Relocation Center where she was being detained by the army. *Ex Parte Mitsuye Endo*, 123 U.S. 283 (1944). Unlike Korematsu, the government in *Endo* conceded that Endo was a loyal American citizen, and the Court held that the president's executive order could not have intended to authorize detention of admittedly loyal Japanese Americans.
6.   Ibid., 242.
7.   *Korematsu v. United States*, 584 F. Supp 1406 (N.D. Cal. 1984).
8.   See *Langton and Leblank v. Hogan, et al.*, 71 F.3d 930 (CA. 1st, 1995); *Souza v. Travisono*, 498 F.2d 1120 (CA. 1st, 1974); *Smith v. Robbins*, 454 F.2d 696 (CA. 1st, 1972).
9.   392 U.S. 1 (1968).
10.   Brian Glick, *War at Home: Covert Action against U.S Activists and What We Can Do about It* (Boston: South End Press, 1989).
11.   Ibid.
12.   Senate Report 101–46 at 2 (1989).
13.   Poindexter's conviction was reversed by the U.S Court of Appeals for the D.C. Circuit on the ground that his immunized testimony before Congress was indirectly used against him at his trial.
14.   Editorial, "And a Victory for Liberty," *Hartford Courant*, 7 March 2003, p. A10.
15.   Philip B. Heymann, *Terrorism and America: A Commonsense Strategy for a Democratic Society* (Cambridge, Mass.: MIT Press, 1998), 105.

Index

About the Author

Samuel Dash, a professor at Georgetown University Law Center, is a leading lawyer and scholar in constitutional criminal justice and professional responsibility. He was district attorney of Philadelphia, as well as a criminal defense lawyer. He is best known for his work as chief counsel of the U.S. Senate Watergate Committee, which led to the resignation of President Richard Nixon. He has also been active in international human rights matters, in one case helping to mediate the release of Nelson Mandela from prison. He has two grown daughters, Judi-Ellen and Rachel, and lives with his wife, Sara, in Chevy Chase, Maryland.